The Developing Child

Recent decades have witnessed unprecedented advances in research on human development. Each book in The Developing Child series reflects the importance of this research as a resource for enhancing children's well-being. It is the purpose of the series to make this resource available to that increasingly large number of people who are responsible for raising a new generation. We hope that these books will provide rich and useful information for parents, educators, child-care professionals, students of developmental psychology, and all others concerned with childhood.

Jerome Bruner, University of Oxford
Michael Cole, Rockefeller University
Barbara Lloyd, University of Sussex
Series Editors

Play

Catherine Garvey

Harvard University Press
Cambridge, Massachusetts
1977

Library of Congress Cataloging in Publication Data
Garvey, Catherine, 1930-
  Play.
  (The Developing child)
  Bibliography: p.
  Includes index.
  1. Play. I. Title. II. Series. [DNLM: 1. Child
development. 2. Play. WS105 G242p]
HQ782.G34   155.4'18   76-49884
ISBN 0-674-67361-1 (cloth)
ISBN 0-674-67363-8 (paper)

Acknowledgments

Much of the research work for this book was supported by grants from the National Institute of Mental Health (United States Department of Health, Education and Welfare). The cooperation of the several nursery schools and their playful children, who must remain anonymous, is hereby gratefully acknowledged. I am also indebted to Rita Berndt, Sandra Bond, Robert Hogan, Alicia Lieberman, Clementine Kaufman, and Stuart Hulse for their helpful comments on earlier versions of the book. A special note of thanks is owed to Fred, an old but still imaginative cat who taught me a great deal about play.

C. G.

Contents

Credits

The
Developing
Child

Play

1 / What Is Play?

The play of children may strike us at times as fragile and charming, rowdy and boisterous, ingenuous, just plain silly, or disturbingly perceptive in its portrayals of adult actions and attitudes. If we look more closely, however, we can discern patterns of amazing regularity and consistency. My aim in this book is to show child's play in a new way, to show its systematic and rule-governed nature, which is, at once, the product and the trace of man's biological heritage and his culture-creating capacity. Play is most frequent in a period of dramatically expanding knowledge of self, the physical and social world, and systems of communication; thus we might expect that play is intricately related to these areas of growth. I am particularly interested in relating the structures of play to the productive uses of language, since both are powerful influences on the child's construction of reality. But let us start at the beginning, with definitions.

An Oxford philosopher, caricatured (or immortalized) in Tom Stoppard's play *Jumpers*, found himself entangled in an exceedingly difficult question: "Does God exist?" he inquired. Realizing that the question was a stubborn one, he tried an often successful rhetorical ploy. He repeatedly rephrased the question, asking next, "What is God?" and finally, ungrammatically but incisively, "What are God?" Let us take up the problem of defining our subject matter with a similar tactic, and pose the question, "What are play?"

Consider this purely imaginary dialogue between a mother and her six-year-old son:

1

> "Tom, I want to clean this room. Go out and play."
> "What do you mean 'go out and play'?"
> "You know what I mean."·
> "No, I don't."
> "Well, just go out and do whatever you do when you're having too much fun to come in to dinner."
> "You mean toss the tennis ball against the garage? Finish painting my bike? Practice standing on my head? Tease Andy's sister? Check out the robin eggs?"

The conclusion of the dialogue, which might involve parental violence, is best omitted.

In everday conversation, it is generally unfair and provoking to ask for precise definitions of familiar words. But when a familiar concept like aggression, intelligence, or personality becomes an object of study, then it must be defined or delineated, at least clearly enough so that those who contribute to the study and those who may benefit from it know they are talking about the same thing. Play has been a particularly recalcitrant notion, but we must try to specify what the term means—at least as it is used in the following pages.

An infant shaking a rattle again and again, a kitten chasing its tail, a group of boys absorbed in a game of marbles, a girl preparing an elaborate feast for the inhabitants of a doll's house, a toddler gleefully running from its mother, girls skipping rope to a rhymed chant, a child finger painting, two monkeys taking turns at attacking and fleeing, a little boy spanking and scolding his stuffed bear—are all these events play? What characteristics do they have in common? Is there any feature unique to play? Is play in childhood related to adult play? to the play of young animals?

In everyday use of the term the central notion seems clear enough, but the fringes of the concept are fuzzy. Play, like Proteus, keeps changing shape. Different scholars have fastened on one or two of its characteristic forms and have offered a variety of theories to account for the origins, properties, and functions of these forms in the life of the individual or the group. For example, the fact that, almost universally, the young of higher species engage in playful behavior that resembles adult activities but is somehow incomplete or unperfected led one scholar to propose that play was instinctive, its function being to exercise skills necessary for adult life. Karl Groos, a philosopher, saw in the play-fighting of animals and the imitative behavior of children a preparation for adult performance. A psychologist, G. Stanley Hall, noting the same characteristics as well as the fact that playful behavior changes with age, proposed the "recapitulation" theory. This maintained that the play of children reflects the course of evolution from prehistoric hominids to the present. The history of the race is recapitulated in each child's development. Both theories were developed at the turn of the century and were heavily influenced by Darwin's concept of natural selection.

Sheer exuberance is another seemingly universal characteristic of much playful behavior. The young of higher species frolic, frisk, gallop, gambol, cavort, engage in mock combat, with every sign of pleasure and high spirits and with no apparent utilitarian objective. These boisterous forms of play suggested to Herbert Spencer an expenditure of surplus energy. In one of the earliest books on psychology, Spencer hypothesized that excess energy accumulates (as a normal product of the healthy nervous system) and must then be discharged. Where no pressing demand is made for survival (in hunting, fighting, or mating) the superabundance of energy is released in exercises that employ normal patterns of behavior but lack any immediate goal. Spencer attempted to specify a physiological process that could explain this aspect of play and to account not only for its presence in higher forms of life but for its manifestations in individual species as well.

These explanations—instinctive preparation, recapitulation, and surplus energy—have since been discarded or revised and adapted to more current theoretical positions, but the phenomena they attempted to explain (partial similarity to adult behavior, gradual acquisition of new forms of play, exuberant activity) are important aspects of play. And there are yet other aspects that have attracted investigators from different scientific and humanistic areas. For example, the fact that in pretending children often express indirectly or symbolically pressing worries or fears and repeat these themes again and again suggests a view of play as cathartic—an attempt to reexperience, and thereby to resolve or master, a difficult situation. This aspect of play has been of particular interest to psychiatrists and clinical psychologists.

The diversity of forms of play coupled with the different approaches to its study has led to a proliferation of ideas concerning the causes of play and the functions it may serve. However, basic to any theoretical position that attempts to answer questions concerning its causes or its role in the life of any creature, species, or society is the specification of the phenomenon in question. Succinctly put by Hughlings Jackson: "The study of the causes of things must be preceded by the study of the things caused." Accordingly, in this book I will describe the various aspects of young children's play before offering speculations about its causes or its functions in the course of development.

Certain descriptive characteristics of play are widely cited as critical to its definition. Most students of play would accept the following inventory:

(1) Play is pleasurable, enjoyable. Even when not actually accompanied by signs of mirth, it is still positively valued by the player.

(2) Play has no extrinsic goals. Its motivations are instrinsic and serve no other objectives. In fact, it is more an enjoyment of means than an effort devoted to some particular end. In utilitarian terms, it is inherently unproductive.

(3) Play is spontaneous and voluntary. It is not obligatory but is freely chosen by the player.

(4) Play involves some active engagement on the part of the player.

Each of these characteristics is partially typical of states other than play. Work or artistic endeavors are frequently pleasurable and often undertaken spontaneously, but both have a product of some sort: each is intended to change the real world in some perceptible way. The same is true of organized sports, especially professional or competitive sports. Lounging is often pleasurable, freely undertaken, and quite often has no specific goal (though one may rest in order to recuperate or just to avoid working). But it does not require active engagement. Just doing nothing, being bored, is usually not pleasurable. It neither engages the person nor has a predetermined product, though the state may be voluntary. Daydreaming is often conceived of as pleasurable and is usually voluntary, but the daydreamer is passive, not actively engaged.

The final item on the inventory of widely accepted characteristics is:

(5) Play has certain systematic relations to what is not play.

This last quality is the most intriguing one. If play were just a unique, isolated outcropping, a widespread but temporary and harmless aberration of childhood, then it would be interesting as a fact, perhaps, but the study of play would have little redeeming scientific value. However, play has been linked with creativity, problem solving, language learning, the development of social roles, and a number of other cognitive and social phenomena. The need to specify the nature of these links continues to motivate research.

The systematic relationships of play to what is not play carry an important implication that will be developed throughout this book. In fact, the very idea of play depends on contrast. We can only speak of play when we can contrast it with other orientations or states; we can only identify playful behavior when the actor can and does engage in corresponding but contrasting nonplayful behavior. The notion of contrast between play and nonplay and the fact that there are certain similarities between playful behavior and analogous nonplay behavior have influenced recent attempts to arrive at a working definition of play. It has become increasingly clear within the last decade that it is impossible to define play as a particular type or set of actions. Jumping, throwing a stone, chasing someone, even asking a question, or imitating another person's speech or movements can be performed as play but can also, of course, be performed in a nonplay fashion and with nonplayful intent. Some approach other than a simple inventory of play activities is obviously required.

One proposal has been made by Peter Reynolds, a specialist on the behavior of rhesus monkeys. He has suggested that play be considered "behavior in the simulative mode."[1] He observed that his monkey subjects displayed few action patterns (chase, present, mount, grab, or lunge) only in play and that few such patterns failed to occur in play. Taking into account the types of criteria used to identify and classify animal behavior (for example, physiological function, physical appearance, underlying mechanism in the nervous system, and effects on the environment), he suggested that behavior is organized into complex patterns he called "affective-behavioral systems." These are complexes of behavior, each one with its characteristic objectives and emotional orientations and typical outcomes. Feeding and mating are examples of such systems. Each system is linked to certain other systems—for instance, courtship normally precedes mating. When an affective-behavioral system (such as aggressive attack) is temporarily uncoupled from its usual relations to other systems, but still operates normally in respect to its own internal dynamics, it is functioning in the simulative mode. Play is an affective-behavioral system in its own right. It has, however, no particular behavior or objective unique to itself. Its behavior patterns are "borrowed" from other affective-behavioral systems. Thus, when the aggressive-attack system is transferred to the simulative mode for actual performance, the resulting behavior *resembles* a purposive attack. But the attacker performs his play-attack outside the context that might normally instigate attack, and he does not carry it through to its typical end. Reynolds suggests that simulation provides savings in both physiological and psychological energy to the young animal, and Jerome Bruner has also stressed the advantages of performances that are free, or "buffered," from normal consequences.[2]

In identifying an activity pattern as one performed in the simulative mode, we must necessarily rely on *contrasts* between the simulation and the behavior from which it derives. The contrasts may often be quite subtle—a fleeting grin or a quick wink may accompany an otherwise stinging verbal insult. Indeed, if we watch members of another species or culture, we may miss the contrast until we learn more about the system of communication within which it functions. Human beings tend to interpret behavior even as they see it. They assign meaning to behavior, classify it into conventionalized categories. It is these acts of categorization that permit behavior to be seen as meaningful, as I have proposed in another essay.[3] For example, if we see someone running and another person running a short way behind him, we would probably see these events as related and say that the first person was being chased by the second or that he was fleeing from the second. We might use other behavioral clues to infer guilt or anger on the part of the runners, to decide perhaps that one was a thief, and thus construct a "reasonable explanation" of their actions. This interpretation represents a *literal* orientation to the scene. (It might be changed to another literal interpretation if the next second we saw a rhinoceros charge around a corner after the runners.) But what if we heard one of the runners laugh or noted that they were smiling? Then we would likely decide that we were not witnessing a "real" pursuit, but that they were playing—or "just" playing, as we usually put it. We would have attributed a *nonliteral* orientation to the runners and constructed a nonliteral interpretation of what we saw. And just as we attribute meaning or intent to the actions of others, we conceive of our own behavior in similar terms: we interpret our actions and feelings as belonging to the same categories of intention, attitudes, and purposes, and entering into the same means-ends relationships, that we use to interpret the actions of others.

All play requires the players to understand that what is done is not what it appears to be. It is this nonliteral attitude that allows play to be buffered from its consequences: in effect, it permits play to be play. If play is a nonliteral orientation and playful behavior reflects that orientation, then we can ask: orientation to what, exactly?

RESOURCES FOR PLAY

Adult play is often quite complex, and several layers of significance may be present simultaneously. Further, much of what adults would call play has become "institutionalized"; there are fairly rigorous guidelines for selecting who may do it, when and where it is permissible, or how it is to be done. It is beyond the scope of this book to trace play forms through to adolescence or adulthood, but we may suppose that the aspects of play discussed below can exist even after childhood.

One widely accepted way of cutting up the universe of play makes the divisions at points where major changes in the child's growth become evident. Jean Piaget has divided play into three types.[4] Sensorimotor play, the first type, occupies the period from infancy through to the second year of life, when the child is busy acquiring control over his movements and learns to coordinate his gestures and his perception of their effects. Play at this stage often consists of repeating and varying motions. The infant derives pleasure from mastering motor skills and from experimenting with the world of touch and sight and sound. He takes joy in being able to cause events to recur. Symbolic or representational play is the second type, predominating after the age of two to about six. During this period a child acquires the ability to encode his experiences in symbols; images of events can be recalled. A child begins to play with symbols and their combinations, pretending, perhaps, to fill a nest with eggs as he piles marbles in a doll's hat. The third type of play is games with rules, which begins with the school years. The child has begun to understand certain social concepts of cooperation and competition; he is beginning to be able to work and to think more objectively. His play reflects this change as he is drawn to games that are structured by objective rules and may involve team or group activities.

This book, like some current work that will be discussed, departs from Piaget's formulation in two ways. In the first place I will examine specific types of play behavior and trace them through their lines of development. In the second, in contrast to approaches that stress the relation of play to the major changes in individual cognitive development, I emphasize the social nature of play from its beginnings: play with others is primary, and solitary play and private fantasy are secondary, derived ways of playing. The origins of most of the aspects of play can be detected, as I will attempt to show, in the earliest contacts of the child with his parents or caregivers. Although new ways of playing may be learned gradually and in other contexts, a nonliteral orientation to experiences is probably communicated to an infant within the first months of life.

Play takes many forms. One way of looking at its various aspects is to consider what material or resource is central: With what exactly is the child engaged? If it is true that a child can treat nonliterally whatever he has become familiar with—though not necessarily mastered—then new resources for play should appear as his world expands and becomes differentiated. It should be the case that as new abilities enter the repertoire through maturation or learning, or both, they become playable. As meaningful experiences are distinguished, they can be treated in a nonliteral fashion.

We will look at the aspects of play one by one, distinguishing them by the material or resource primarily involved. These resources are actually classes of experiences. They include motion and changes in perception resulting primarily from physical movement; objects and their physical as well as their combinational or associational properties; language and speech, which offer many levels of organization that can be turned to play; social materials, such as roles, situations, and attitudes—the various notions concerning the way the social world is constructed; and finally limits, where following rules or consciously breaking them is the primary resource for play. These aspects, the way they emerge and develop, their possible combination and integration into complex episodes of play, are my central topics.

RESEARCH PROCEDURES

Many examples of play in the following chapters are derived from an observational study of pairs of children in a single setting. The procedures were designed to provide examples of spontaneous behavior as little constrained as possible but in a setting that was the "same" for all the children. The principal objective of the study was a detailed analysis of children's activities in what was, potentially at least, a social situation. We asked these questions: To what extent do children interact with their peers in the absence of an adult? How does a child communicate with an agemate—that is, how is their conversation constructed? If the pair engages in social play, how exactly is it conducted?

These questions were formulated against a background of research that had emphasized the initial egocentrism of the preschool child in his thought and in his social life. During this period and up to the age of about eight, a child gradually "decenters." He becomes increasingly able to take the perspective of other persons, to understand not only that they may perceive, feel, and think differently from the way he does, but also to interpret their actions in different situations and to arrive at an understanding of what they may perceive, feel, or think. His actions and perceptions become less and less self-referenced. He learns to interact with people outside his family. He gradually moves from being a loner in play and work toward cooperation and teamwork.

Although this picture of the child is in some respects accurate, it is now apparent that emphasis on an understanding of decentering processes led researchers to neglect or ignore the social impulses and abilities that the child does actually possess—even at the very time that he can be accurately characterized as limited by his self-centeredness. But quite recently investigations have begun to search for the beginnings of children's discrimination of emotions in others, for the precursors of reciprocal, interpersonal communication, for the techniques whereby children engage and maintain interactions with their peers, and for the conditions under which children can accurately assess the perspective of another person. One example will indicate this shift in focus. From observations of children's behavior in a nursery school, Piaget noted that relatively little of the children's talk could be classified as "adapted" conversation—that is, as talk designed for and responsive to the informational needs of a particular listener. The children did not talk with one another so much as they engaged in noncommunicative repetitions, soliloquies, or collective monologuing, when everyone talked and no one listened. About 40 percent of four-year-olds' speech was found to be "egocentric," that proportion decreasing with age. In subsequent studies it has been shown that with age a child becomes increasingly better able to take his listener's needs into account.

A shift in research focus takes place when we ask: What about the other side of the coin? If 40 percent of the young child's speech is noncommunicative, what about the remaining 60 percent? Does adapted conversation resemble the speech of more mature speakers, or are children's conversations qualitatively different from those of skilled conversationalists? In respect to objective information exchange, we may ask: If the child does become more skilled in conveying information appropriate to the needs of his listener, how is it that even in his relatively unskilled period he manages to interact effectively, at least in some situations? What kind of "information" does he first learn to convey effectively, and under what conditions does improvement in communication skills first appear? In effect, the shift of emphasis reflects a renewed interest in the behavior of children as children, and it was in this climate of investigation that the work to be described here was undertaken.

We asked five private nursery schools serving a middle-class population in an eastern American city to select several sets of three children. Members of a set were of approximately the same age; were from the same class (and thus were acquainted with each other and the nursery school to much the same extent); and came from English-speaking homes. Each set was made up of either two girls and one boy or two boys and one girl. In all, forty-eight children took part in this study: four sets aged 2 years 10 months to 3 years 3 months (six girls and six boys); four, 3:6 to 4:4 (six girls and six boys); and eight, 4:7 to 5:7 (fifteen girls and nine boys).

Each set of three, accompanied by a nursery-school teacher, was welcomed by a young female researcher who escorted them to an office and relieved them of coats and boots. The researcher took the children to the water fountain and to the toilet and then invited them to draw straws to decide "who would get to go see the playroom first and who would get to play some games first." The child who drew the long straw went to another room with a young male researcher where he was given simple discrimination tasks and encouraged to talk about the miniature objects and pictures, or just to draw pictures if he preferred. The remaining two children were shown into the room where they would be observed. The pair of children was then left alone, and the teacher and researchers watched them from another room through one-way mirrors. A few sessions were briefly interrupted for a potty break or, if a child appeared concerned over the whereabouts of the teacher, to assure him that she was busy but would be along in a few minutes. Each pair remained in the room for about fifteen minutes. Then the third child was brought to the room, and one member of the pair turned to the discrimination tasks. In this way three pairs were formed in succession, and each child was observed with two different agemates.

The room in which the pairs were observed was furnished with a sofa, round movable table, carpet, curtains at the "windows," and bright pictures on the walls. In its center was a wooden box large enough for two children to sit on. It had a real automobile steering wheel and license plate, with four wheels painted on. Over this car was the microphone, which hung from a parrot on a perch. Placed about the room were a stool with a magnifying glass in the center; toy cars and trucks, ironing board and iron, stove with oven, dishes and pans, broom, toolbelt with pliers, hammer, and so on; a large stuffed snake, bear, fish, and tiger, a baby doll and cradle, blocks; a large cardboard box, suitcases, pocketbook, and lunchbox, all concealing jewelry, hats, shoes, shawls; and paper and colored pencils.

Each session was videotaped; all speech was transcribed in standard orthography, and a narrative account of the concurrent nonverbal behavior was prepared. Utterances (defined as stretches of one person's speech separated by the speech of the partner or separated by a pause exceeding one second) were numbered for ease of reference.

An interesting observation was made at the time of data collection. After the first two sets had visited the laboratory, we realized that, during the reception period, not one of the three children had spoken directly to another child, though most children talked quite freely with the adult researchers and the teacher. They did talk about one another, for instance "Johnny has a birthday today," but addressed their comments and questions about the new setting exclusively to the adults. Thereafter the researcher who welcomed the children carried a small tape recorder in her pocketbook during the reception period—to toilet, water fountain, and while getting coats off and on. We confirmed our initial impression, which was all the more striking in contrast with the extensive conversations that took place between the children themselves in the playroom. It appeared that the availability of adults had restricted the children's conversation with one another.

A second body of observations of agemates has been collected with similar procedures by Alicia Lieberman at the Johns Hopkins University. There were several ways in which the procedures and children used in her study differed from the study just described. Pairs (rather than triads) of same-sex, previously unacquainted children came to the laboratory at the same time. Half the subjects attended full-time day-care centers; half, part-time nursery schools. After their reception at the laboratory, however, the observation procedures, room, and furnishings were essentially the same. There were forty children in this study ranging in age from 3:0 to 3:6. The main objective of the research was to study individual differences in preschoolers' social competence when interacting with an unfamiliar child.

The majority of examples in this book are derived from my own work described above, but some are taken from the sessions collected by Lieberman. I will identify examples from both studies as "paired age-mate sessions" when it is necessary to distinguish them from illustrative material taken from other research. When comparisons between the behavior of the acquainted pairs and the unacquainted pairs are relevant, the two types of groups will be identified as such.

Analyses of the data derived from the acquainted pairs support the following conclusions:

(1) Pairs of children as young as three years were able to sustain a conversational interaction, though the length of such exchanges tended to increase with age. There were more episodes of focused interaction, that is—of mutual attending and responsiveness—than would be expected from the previous reports of solitary or parallel play in nursery schools. A number of conversation-building techniques were well controlled by even the youngest pairs. For example, one of these techniques is the ability to convey a request (A: *Give me that hammer*); express noncompliance (B: *I got it first*); paraphrase the unsuccessful request (A: *Well, I need it*); and negotiate the demand (B: *You can have the pliers.* A: *No, I'll give you the flashlight if you give me the hammer*).

A technique that was used for clarifying a misheard or a misunderstood utterance involved precise control of intonation. When one child didn't hear what the other had said, he would ask, ′What or ′Huh,* and thereby elicit a repetition from the other. If he failed to understand some part of the message he could ask ʼWhat or ʼWho and receive the specific information he needed. To compare these two common and essential procedures, consider these contrasting examples:

A: It doesn't work.	A: It doesn't work.
B: ′What?	B: ʼWhat?
A: It doesn't work.	A: The iron.

In the following chapters examples of play will illustrate many other ways in which the children exhibited conversational skills.

*Direction of pitch is indicated by a symbol placed immediately before the syllable that initiates a pitch change. ʼand ˎ indicate high falling and low falling pitch; ′and ˏ , high rising and low rising; and ⌢and ⌄ indicate high rising-falling and low rising-falling pitch, respectively. Conventional punctuation is retained, though it is usually redundant given the pitch symbols.

(2) There was considerable variation in a child's social behavior depending in part on the behavior and compatibility of his partner. With a less talkative partner a child would speak less than he did with his other more loquacious partner. The success of play episodes also varied across pairs. Two children might jointly construct several complex make-believe episodes, but when one of the children was paired with his second partner, make-believe play might be fragmentary or virtually nonexistent. Further, the teachers reported that many of the children seemed far more peer-oriented and socially skilled in the agemate sessions than at the nursery school or on the playground. Two factors may contribute to this effect: the absence of an adult and the reduction of the social and physical distractions generally found in nursery-school classes. It is likely that a pair comprises the most natural of social units. Basic patterns of exchange are first learned in the mother-infant pair. It may be that one must then *learn* to interact with more than one person at a time and must acquire techniques for dealing with persons whose speech and conversational habits are not well known. And in the laboratory playroom there was no distracting noise or interruption from other children's activities, which there clearly are even in the best-run nursery class or play group.

(3) Perhaps the most important result to emerge from this study is the overwhelming evidence that *not all that young children do together is play.* They have many modes of interacting, and they mark the play mode as distinct from other orientations. This may seem obvious on first reading since it is well known that children also fight and argue or often just watch each other. However, like many "obvious" facts this has been widely ignored, and we have as one consequence little information about how children actually do communicate with other children or transact their social affairs. The fact that the children in the paired agemate sessions moved back and forth among different activities and often changed their orientation to each other was most important, since it provided clear and often striking contrasts on which to base the descriptions of play as opposed to other orientations.

It has been proposed that the first functional distinction regarding the use of language is that between speaking and keeping silent. After that, of course, many other distinctions are made—

those that determine the choice of polite, humorous, or condescending alternatives for speaking and acting, and so on. One of the first functional discriminations in the perception of persons is, most probably, that of familiar and unfamiliar. After that, such distinctions as age, sex, and status are made and become more and more influential in determining choices among the available variants in the child's repertoire of behavior. From examination of the videotapes made of the sessions we extracted two very critical distinctions that appear to influence almost everything a child does. We would expect these distinctions to be made and used at a very early age, but certainly by the age of three most children are able to verbalize their awareness of whether they are playing or not and of whether they are alone or are engaged with another person. Almost all of the videotaped data could be classified into the four possible states that result from the distinctions: play/nonplay and social/nonsocial. In other words, a child could be playing or not playing and, in the latter case, he could be doing nothing, or what we might call problem solving, or engaging in talk that was neither playful nor directed toward the solution of any immediate problem or difficulty. The existence of other orientations contributes to the identification of play itself, which is thus marked as a special state. This marking is particularly clear—and critical—when the child is interacting with another child, for in that situation the two must communicate to each other whether what is done is done as play or as nonplay. Successful interaction between children depends on the participants' mutual awareness of whether they are playing or not playing. The paired agemate sessions provide a situation in which the intimate relationship between play and communication is strikingly evident.

My examination of play in childhood begins with a brief discussion of the emergence of smiling and laughter, which are common though not essential signals of a playful orientation. The following chapters describe five aspects of play distinguished according to the resource with which the child is primarily engaged—for instance, motion, objects, or language. Next I discuss a very special way of playing, with rules and rituals. Finally, I conclude with a summary of the major points and with some proposals concerning the functions of play in childhood.

2 / The Natural History of the Smile

The development of smiling parallels that of play. Compared to play, however, smiling has a fairly constant form. It can be observed, described, and reliably identified; it can be elicited and its immediate antecedents can be manipulated in order to determine what encourages or discourages its appearance. What is known about smiling mirrors some of the important characteristics of play.

An infant's first smiles are faint and fleeting and appear in the absence of any external stimulation. Endogenous, or internally triggered, smiles occur primarily during sleep and are believed to reflect mild changes in physiological excitation. A clearer, more positive smile in response to external stimulation (the exogenous smile) begins to appear in waking states at about three weeks of age. This smile, which is marked by crinkling around the eyes as well as a broader upturning of the lips, reflects the infant's attention to changes in his environment. However, the stimulation must be relatively mild or he will startle. What elicits a smile—that is, the type, intensity, and complexity of the stimulation—changes with maturation. During the third week of life it is the female voice that is most consistently effective. After the first month an infant will indicate his pleased attention at a silent moving face. Soon after the second month most infants will smile broadly at a round of Pat-a-Cake.

Not long after the exogenous smile appears, there is evidence that an infant begins to participate actively in creating and sustaining the states of stimulation that lead to smiling. What strikes him as amusing now appears to involve not only sound or motion as such but some contrast between expectation and perception. A familiar phenomenon, distorted or exaggerated in some way, now elicits smiles or laughter. Mother walking like a penguin or wearing a mask is funny, and repetition of such events usually produces a smile or a laugh. The timing of these responses indicates anticipation of the previously experienced outcome. An older infant is willing and able to participate in producing humor. The conditions under which he does so indicate the rapidly increasing role of his own interpretation and evaluation of potentially amusing events. According to Alan Sroufe, a psychologist who has traced this development of smiling and laughter through the first year of life, an infant tends to be attracted to the incongruous—what he does not quite understand. If he can interpret a novel event as nonthreatening, then he will laugh or smile. As he matures, he becomes increasingly active in producing and mastering new experiences that generate amusement.[1]

The smile grows from a faint grimace to a broad grin. Chortles, laughs, chuckles, and guffaws come later but do not, of course, replace smiling. What elicits such responses becomes increasingly differentiated until by early childhood a number of different classes of events are effective. In what may be one of the most delightful experiments in the history of psychology (a discipline not usually given to amusing treatment of its subject matter), Florence Justin attempted in 1932 to discover the immediate causes for laughter in children.[2] She set out to test various theories of the antecedents of laughter, among which were theories that laughter resulted from surprise or a defeated expectation; a feeling of superiority at another's misfortune or ineptness; release from strain or tension; perception of incongruity and contrast; seeing another person laugh or indicate that something was funny; and engaging in verbal or physical play.

Justin's techniques for eliciting laughter from children aged three, four, five, and six were ingenious. For example, interviewing one child at a time amid a number of props, she announced that she would boil an egg in a pan of water and time it with a watch. Then she dropped the watch in the hot water and consulted the egg. Next she invited the child to join her for a story session, pulled up a small chair, started to sit down, missed the chair, and tumbled onto the floor. These happenings were used to test the superiority-degradation theory. To test the surprise theory, she presented three little covered buckets. The child inserted his hand through a slit to find sand in one, water in the next, and in the third, nothing. To test the strain theory, a child walked a narrow line carrying a parasol and a potato in a spoon. The social smile was elicited by the experimenter smiling and laughing herself, tacitly inviting a response by the child.

Justin found that all the conditions elicited smiling or laughter from each age group. From 40 to 95 percent of the children in each group smiled in each of the situations, but older children responded to a greater variety of incidents and tended to smile longer. According to the length of the responses and to the percentage of children giving a response to each condition, relief from strain or tension and superiority-degradation were least effective. The social-smile situation was highly effective, even for the three-year-olds. There was a slight tendency for children to laugh more at situations in which they participated directly. Justin's study suggests that by the age of three most adult forms of mirth are foreshadowed but that "the field of the laughable is being constantly extended." She attributed the enlargement of the field of laughter-provoking incidents to the processes of mental growth.

Investigation of the immediate contexts of smiles and laughter in the paired agemate sessions of acquainted children suggests that at least as many types of conditions are effective in producing spontaneous humor responses as those used by Florence Justin. Further, laughter or giggles also appeared to serve such social functions as attracting a partner's attention, enticing him to join in some activity, or marking what one had just done as "funny." There were several instances in which an apparently aggressive gesture (like snatching an object from a partner or threatening with raised arm and clenched fist) was accompanied by exaggerated laughter. In these cases the marker of playful intent was generally effective in that the partner did not respond defensively. For the preschool age child, then, smiles and laughter have become an important part of the complex system of signals he can send and interpret when interacting with others.

Smiling is universal in our species, which has been called *homo ludens.* * It would follow that smiling has some physiological basis and that it plays or has played some role in the evolu-

---

*There is some question as to whether anthropoids smile, although a smilelike expression has been observed under certain conditions in apes, most notably when they were watching young human children.

tion of the species. The psychophysiological basis for the smile is thought to be a process of tension-relaxation. This happens when the infant encounters something novel or unusual. First he freezes and gives it all his attention. Then, if he finds it threatening or unpleasant, he will cry or perhaps move away; if not, the tension evaporates and he will smile, laugh, or perhaps even approach or reach out. The important point here is that it is his *evaluation* of the event, person, or object as interesting but not threatening that tips the balance toward smiling or laughter.

Studies of smiling and laughter have shown that infants and young children are sensitive to various dimensions of social settings. Researchers have found that, while laughter would be elicited at five weeks in the home, it could not be called forth in the laboratory until twelve or sixteen weeks. Children of one year would respond to tickling by parents in a laboratory, but would not laugh if tickled by the experimenter. At about the same time the approach of a strange child might elicit a smile, whereas the approach of a strange adult would probably produce some negative reaction.

A young infant's smile on the appearance of its mother has been called a smile of recognition. It begins to appear at about three months and is generally overinterpreted by the mother to mean "he recognizes *me.*" Naturally, this "greeting" evokes a strong maternal response in her. If the expression was instinctive at first, it now enters into a system of social interactions in which the behavior of each participant is influenced by that of the other. It appears that prolonging an infant's smiling or laughter is extremely satisfying for parents. Smiling and laughter, then, have not only evaluative and expressive functions, but are important in initiating and maintaining early communicative exchanges. Adults often work indefatigably to bring forth smiles and laughter in their young, and a healthy baby soon learns how to keep his parents performing in an amusing way. It is increasingly clear that in the infant's early pleasurable encounters he is more than a pleased, passive audience. He actively invites certain diversions and rejects others.

By nursery-school age, a child is able to find many different classes of phenomena amusing or delightful. He has a range of responses—smiling, laughing, giggling—and this range probably reflects the qualitative or quantitative distinctions he can make among amusing events. Further, he can discriminate certain aspects of social situations (setting, and the age, number, and familiarity of the people involved) which influence his evaluation of what is funny and the kind of response he is likely to produce. It is this last fact that has posed problems for investigations of children's understanding and enjoyment of humor. Signs of amusement may be inhibited in an experimental situation and even the stimulus—a joke or cartoon—may elicit a problem-solving approach instead of mirth. Conversely, what is evaluated as funny and the intensity of the overt response can be positively influenced by the social situation. And the threshhold for delight and its expression can be dramatically lowered for children by the sheer presence of other children.

GROUP GLEE

A fascinating phenomenon, long familiar to nursery-school teachers, has recently been discussed and named for the scientific community by Lawrence Sherman.[3] That phenomenon is "group glee," the spontaneous eruption of mirth among children. It manifests itself in a sudden wave of screams or giggles, and often involves jumping up and down and hand-clapping. It appears to possess all the children simultaneously or spreads like wildfire from one child through the group. Over a two-year period, Sherman observed 596 directed-activity sessions lasting about twenty minutes. Group size in the nursery school was small (three to four), medium (five to six), and large (seven to nine). The sessions were made up of children of the ages of three, four, and five. In all, 633 outbreaks of group glee were observed.

The immediate antecedents of group glee, Sherman found, were quite varied. Four were similar to the antecedents of laughter: intense physical activity such as dancing; an incongruent perception—as when one child called a teddy bear a "teddy dog"; taboo breaking with "bad words," or rule transgression; and perception of another's misfortune—as when one child tripped over a milk carton. However, other events or situations could also trigger group glee. The most effective of these were volunteering—for example, the teacher asked "Who wants to go outside and get John?" and the children shouted "Me, me me . . ."; termination of a situation, such as the end of a story session; announcement of a future event; and unstructured situations—as when children were left waiting before a planned activity began. An episode of group glee is likely to last less than nine seconds and tends to occur more frequently in the larger groups and in mixed rather than in same-sex groups. All age groups engaged in this behavior to about the same extent. (Teachers acted to suppress gleeful explosions when these occurred during a lesson activity and particularly when they *spread* throughout the group [rather than erupting simultaneously in the entire group]. Otherwise they generally tolerated them.)

Do experiences of group glee in a nursery class contribute to learning and retention of lesson materials, or to the willingness of the classmates to cooperate with the teacher and with each other? One might speculate that the answer would be yes.

Although smiles and laughter are overt behavior, whereas play is an attitude or orientation that can manifest itself in numerous different kinds of behavior, this brief account of smiling, laughter, and glee reveals many similarities to the development of play. First, from early vague gestures, the signs of mirth become increasingly differentiated and clear. Similarly, it is difficult to be quite sure that many infant activities reflect a playful orientation. Probably a very young child is himself not consistently aware of the distinction between play and nonplay in many of his own activities. Certainly he often fails to perceive that distinction in other people's activities. Second, just as a child becomes more active in creating the conditions for a humor response, so does he become more active in play—moving, for example, from an audience role in Peek-a-Boo to an active role by covering his own or his mother's face. In smiling and in playing, the growth of voluntary control is reflected in important changes in the organization of behavior. Third, as a child grows, so does the field of the risible; the nature of what can be appreciated becomes more complex, more varied, and more intellectual. What can be played expands as new areas of experience are encountered and appropriated for playful purposes. Fourth, laughter as a sign of joy and play behavior are both likely to appear under conditions of well-being. The sick, bewildered, frightened child does not smile or play.

Fifth, and finally, smiling and playing come under the influence of social and environmental factors virtually from their beginnings. Both are highly social in their earliest periods and are shaped thereafter by interpersonal and environmental contingencies. Both smiling and playing are implicated in the child's first experiences of mutually shared attention and awareness with his parents and become more and more systematically linked with communicative exchanges. Through childhood and beyond, smiling and playing continue to have important ties with social phenomena; their occurrence is in part dependent on social factors such as familiarity and group size. Further, many aspects of children's play are also sensitive to the sex composition of the group.

Thus there are several interesting parallels between play and the development of smiling and laughter. But a word of caution is necessary. Not all manifestations of play are marked by grins or giggles, and a smile is by no means a reliable index of a playful orientation. It is characteristic of human behavior that there are few, if any, simple and constant relations between a gesture and its meaning or significance in a communicative situation.

3 / Play with Motion and Interaction

The kind of play that most clearly reflects exuberance and high spirits is based on the resource of motion. The running, jumping, skipping, shrieking, and laughing of children at recess or after school is joyous, free, and almost contagious in its expression of well-being. Although it is an aspect of play that has received considerable study, a number of unanswered questions remain. One concerns the development of play with motion in its solitary appearances and in its more boisterous manifestations in groups.

Motion, the sensations of movement and the changing sensations that motion produces, are the first amusements adults offer to infants. Babies are jiggled up and down on the knee, tickled or repeatedly hoisted high in the air, and they show evident signs of pleasure in such experiences. And motion and changing sensations are also the first resources for play that an infant himself can exploit alone during the time he is discovering his ability to control his movements. Piaget provides an example of a solitary infant's discovery of a voluntary movement—tilting his head back. At first the baby used this movement to provide a new view of familiar things but thereafter used his achievement playfully. In Piaget's words, the infant "seemed to repeat this movement with ever-increasing enjoyment and ever-decreasing interest in the external result: he brought his head back to the upright position and then threw it back again time after time, laughing loudly."[1] Such early episodes have in common with later and diverse types of play the fact that they are enjoyed for their own sake and are divorced from other goals they might normally serve.

There are problems in identifying segments of infant behavior as playful. Few of a young infant's movements are sufficiently well controlled to provide clear contrasts between accidental and voluntary behavior. One generally infers that an exchange between an infant and an adult is playful on the basis of their combined behavior. The repetition of movements and displacement of a particular movement from its normal role in a seemingly purposeful sequence of activity are the criteria most often cited as criteria for infant play. By late infancy or early childhood, sequences of skilled movements have developed and can be repeated or shifted from their usual place in a sequence. Furthermore, children have learned how to signal their playful attitude more clearly. Taken together, these developments permit more reliable identification of play.

Not even in the first four months, however, does an infant receive playful adult attention *passively*. Entertainment through motion and sensation may be offered by parents, but the infant takes part. The early play of an infant and its parent has an intrinsic goal that Daniel Stern has described as "pure interaction."[2] The means by which parents can create and maintain an optimal level of attention and arousal in an infant (whose obvious signals of pleasure further promote their efforts) consist of sounds, facial expressions, and movements, often including physical contact. A parent can vary these in speed, intensity, scope, and combination, producing changing and varied sensations. Close observations of infant and parent together suggest that elements of the parent's repertoire become grouped into distinctive, repeatable sequences—some of which can be named, like Pat-a-Cake. Within these sequences, the speed, range, and intensity of the parent's actions are to a large extent controlled by the infant's behavior. The infant's behavior is that action he can best control, his direction of gaze.* He averts his gaze or directs it to his parent, thus regulating the amount of stimulation he receives as well as influencing the entertainer's performance.

An older infant soon produces motion and changing sensa-

---

*A very young infant is strongly predisposed to look at his partner's eyes, but this tendency soon becomes part of a system of interaction as well as a means of adjusting his internal state of arousal. Gaze will later serve as an important part of the more mature nonverbal communication systems he will acquire.

tions more directly in explorations of his environment. As an action pattern is "discovered," it is liable to be repeated and exercised, both for the pleasure of the experience and also to test and extend its immediate consequences. These playful explorations with motion, insofar as they have been described, do not appear to be shared with agemates until well into the second year of life. With cooperative and sensitive adults, however, an older infant takes an increasingly active role in playful activities, often initiating a sequence by himself producing the first move of a familiar game. But although play with motion has social roots in the infant-parent pair, it is not shared with agemates for some period of time to come. The earliest systematic studies of social play with motion begin in nursery school at about the age of three, though there is some evidence that still younger children can interact using alternating, repetitive patterns of physical actions, such as following and leading or imitating one another's movements.

ANIMALS' PLAY

Play involving motion and sensation is of considerable interest in its own right not only because of its prevalence in the healthy child (and thus its probable role in normal development) but also because it is the only aspect of play, to our best knowledge, that is displayed by both animals and human beings. Play in animals has long fascinated naturalists, zoologists, and ethologists. The question of its role in the development of individual animals and of species, in socialization processes and in the ecology of the group, is being researched with renewed interest. It is not surprising that recent study of children's spontaneous physical activities has been conducted primarily with procedures and theoretical orientations from the field of animal ethology. Ethologists believe that play increases the chances of survival for the individual as well as for the group, and that its long-range benefits are best discovered by detailed study of creatures in their natural environment. However, ethologists also arrange, judiciously and with minimal disruption, environmental factors in order to test hypotheses developed from their naturalistic observations.

Irenäus Eibl-Eibesfeldt wrote that "Play is an experimental

dialogue with the environment."[3] Some animals (generally those of "lower species") do not so much conduct a dialogue as follow a set script. Those species that are highly specialized to their specific environments, such as ants or bees, show little, if any, play. Instead play seems to be associated with the potentiality for adapting to changing circumstances. The more flexible an animal is, the more likely it is to play. In fact, Peter Reynolds suggests that a group of phenomena he calls the "flexibility complex" underlies the tendency of the young of a species to play or not. The flexibility complex includes a relatively long period of maturation and dependency on a caregiver, an increased ability to manipulate objects and use them as instruments; an increased reliance on learning by observation—acquiring information from watching others and observing what precedes and follows from their actions; the development of conventional action sequences built on *imitated* behavior; and the development of peer groups in the young and subsequent elaboration of social structures within adolescent subcultures.

The phrase "experimental dialogue" suggests a conversation in which one can take back what is said. Play behavior is, to a considerable extent, revocable. What is done in play is "uncoupled" from the typical consequences of analogous nonplay behavior; thus play provides an opportunity for the relatively safe, or minimally risky, exercise of new behavior in familiar situations, or of familiar behavior in new physical or social contexts. Also, play in animals tends to decline in adolescence and few adults engage in play (except sometimes with their immature young). It is thus likely that the functions of play are closely related to learning and early development. Since the environment is social as well as physical, in addition to integrating their behavior and testing its effect on their physical world, playing animals are learning to "talk" with other members of their groups and to understand one another's signals.

The word "experimental" further suggests curiosity, interest in what is novel or poorly understood. This attitude, sometimes called exploratory, is characteristic of the healthy young of most higher animals. Although we shall see in the next chapter that exploration and play differ in form and conduct, it is nevertheless true that the two are often temporally sequenced. A new experience, if not frightening, is likely first to attract attention, then exploration. Only after a novel feature of the environment has been investigated can it be treated more lightly and enjoyed. In respect to play with motion, there is a close link between exploration and the beginnings of interaction with contemporaries. Agemates are one of the most interesting features of the environment. They differ both from the caregiver and from inanimate things. They attract attention and often investigation because they move and do interesting and unexpected things. Harry Harlow and his colleagues, who have devoted many years to the study of young rhesus monkeys, have observed that play with peers begins as an extension of exploration and play with inanimate objects.[4]

The peak period of play in young animals is more often social than solitary. Since much (though not all) of the behavior exhibited by playing animals also appears later in mature mating, hunting, or fighting, ethologists have emphasized the relations of play to other kinds of action and interaction.* They not only view play as a type of communication but are also interested in the distinctive signals that differentiate playful behavior from the analogous nonplay activities. Thus two basic questions are asked: How do the changing forms of play relate to the life of the animal? How is behavior marked as playful, that is, how is a play orientation communicated within the group?

Two studies of play in animals will illustrate the ethological approach and suggest some ideas concerning the possible functions of play that emerge from this perspective. Meredith West observed twenty-eight domestic cats from fourteen days of age to maturity.[5] Six litters of kittens were kept with their mothers, three litters in a laboratory, and three in a home where they had unlimited access to the outdoors. She also observed three wild mothers and their seven young. During the hour and a half of daily observation, the behavior of each kitten was sampled. Preliminary work resulted in the identification of eight categories of movement patterns. The patterns, themselves complex clusters of behavior, formed the building blocks of longer sequences of

*It is interesting that play is assumed to be possible only among members of the same species, except for man with his pets or animals he has cared for. Few observations have been made of cross-species play, which does occur though only perhaps among domesticated animals who are house, yard, or pasture mates.

interaction. The aptness of the patterns she identified as units is confirmed by their role in the kitten's developing social activity. Briefly, the patterns and the age at which each was first observed were as follows:

Age first seen (in days)	Pattern
33-35	*Pounce.* Crouch with head low; back legs tucked in; hindquarters sway; thrust of forward movement is from extension of hind legs; tail straight back and may move back and forth.
32-34	*Side-step.* Arched back; tail curled up; walks sideways toward or around object or other kitten.
21-23	*Belly-up.* Kitten on back; all paws semi-vertical; hind legs treading, front legs pawing; teeth exposed; tail straight back or may move back and forth.
23-26	*Stand-up.* Stands near or over other kitten, head toward head or neck of other.
42-48	*Face-off.* Sits, hunched forward, eyes oriented to other kitten; lifts front paw forward, tail moves back and forth.
35-38	*Vertical stance.* Sitting position; rocks back on haunches and lifts front paws and stretches them perpendicular to its own body.
41-46	*Horizontal leap.* Lateral position relative to other kitten; back arched, curves tail upward and leaps off ground.
38-41	*Chase.* One kitten runs after (pursuit) or from (flight) another kitten.

These patterns appeared first in a solitary context and some appeared later than others. All were exercised repeatedly as they were first acquired. Then all the patterns began to be joined into sequences, with the number of joined patterns increasing from 4.8 per sequence at six weeks to 8.1 per sequence at twelve weeks.

The most favored opening move in a sequence was the pounce; the second, the side-step. Pounce never ended a bout and was never used as a response to an initial move. Belly-up and stand-up occurred most often in the middle of a sequence, with kittens rapidly exchanging these two complementary positions. Play episodes were usually terminated with a chase. The horizontal leap was the second most frequent termination, but it never started a play bout.

From five weeks play was primarily social. The number of bouts per hour started to increase at five to seven weeks and then from eight to sixteen weeks leveled off at about twelve. Subsequently the amount of social play declined sharply, as did other social activities such as mutual grooming.

A number of changes began to take place around four months of age. The homelife of the kittens began to break up, and they became much more individualistic. They slept more and spent much of their waking time in quiet, alert watching. The house-reared kittens spent most of their time outdoors, exploring and hunting. The males began to display sexual interest at about four and a half months but were rejected and avoided by the females, who did not respond to their advances until five and a half months. Each of the three wild mothers abandoned their kittens at around four months of age, and the littermates who had stayed together in their shelters then began to disperse and to hunt. The changes in play and other behavior were similar for the laboratory cats, who were not forced to obtain their own food and could not roam outdoors. Solitary play also declined, though more slowly, and some of the adults did occasionally play alone with objects.

West points out that several different types of signals can communicate a playful orientation. For example, tail movements in play are broader or more rapid than the analogous movements in neutral or aggressive contexts. Also, though some of the same configurations of movements are used both in play and in fighting, they are structured differently in the two states.

Play is vigorous exercise, it entails close contact with partners and especially one partner at a time, and it declines at the time when litters disperse and the young cats begin to turn their attention to other activities directed to survival (hunting, watching, or mating)—all this indicates that play is an integral and adaptive part of feline development. Since not all feline movement patterns are used in play and since there are also other kinds of social interactions such as grooming, play is by no means the single source of cat expertise, but it does appear to contribute to kittens' social harmony at a time when the litter is dependent on the mother and must stay together.

These observations suggest that play has many functions, and that its forms and periods of predominance are closely tied to the kittens' adaptation to their unique way of life. Some, though not all, of the movement patterns practiced in play are similar to patterns later specialized for hunting and fighting. Other species of animals play in very different ways which are compatible with their particular life style and with their mature nonplay activities. Marc Bekoff's studies of coyotes, beagles, wolves, and hybrids of these animals indicate that, even among these related species, there are striking differences in early social relationships. [6]

Bekoff, like West, developed a list of behavioral components and observed their occurrence and sequence in interactive episodes within pairs of pups. Contrasts between play and nonplay behavior were marked by exaggeration, by different sequences, and by certain movements and vocalizations that occurred uniquely in play. In all the pairs observed, as in the litters of kittens, close contact play preceded running and chasing. But preferred play-initiating moves differed not only from those of the kittens; they also differed among the three species studied.

Beagles were the most playful, wolves somewhat less so, and coyotes played relatively little. As early as twenty-one days of age, coyotes fought seriously. Their social relationships were first established by threatening and fighting, and only thereafter did some play appear. Wolves established their dominance patterns less violently by means of threats and began to play more at about one and a half months of age. Beagles did not engage in fighting, and their organization was quite democratic. Bekoff believes that these patterns of infant interactions are closely related to the beagle's domestication for hunting in groups or packs, to the wolf's cooperative group hunting and living arrangements, and to the coyote's more solitary adult life style.

A favorite beagle play initiation (two or more high leaps directed toward the prospective partner) was also displayed by hybrids derived from mating a coyote or wolf with a domestic dog. All hybrids used leaping as an invitation to play. This pattern has never been observed in coyotes and only rarely in wolves. Hybrids with a wolf parent used leaping more and at an earlier age than did hybrids with a coyote parent. Bekoff also found that the patterns (other than those ending in bouts) were clearly marked as playful. If two apparently conflicting markers occurred together, for example teeth bared (usually a signal of threat) with face-oriented pawing (usually an invitation to play), priority was given to the play signal.

From these two studies, it is clear that communication is an important factor in the social play of animals. Further, the studies support the ideas that play with motion can be reliably identified by contrast with other activity and that, even though species (and breeds) may differ in their forms of signaling, a playful orientation is marked as such. Further, play with motion for most animal species sometimes peaks before maturity, is most often conducted socially, and supports the maintenance of relations among littermates. The existence of specific action patterns, unique to a species, and the different frequency of play between species or breeds suggest a close tie with adult survival behavior and with the life styles of both young and adult animals.

The above also holds true for young primates reared in colonies or in nuclear families with access to others of the same age. As compared with the domestic cats or dogs, primates mature more slowly and remain longer with their mothers; they characteristically begin to play with agemates rather later. For many primates, there is a transitional period from mother-infant relations to playful peer relations. Rhesus monkeys first play alone and begin to contact others at about two months of age, but they take some time to learn how to play together. According to Harlow, their solitary play patterns are the precursors of the numerous interactive play responses that begin to appear after several months. The young rhesus eventually build up complex patterns for social encounters and also display special signals, such as open-mouthed facial expressions and a bounding gait, to indicate their playful orientation. By eight months, play has become the major social activity. Play encounters last longer as age increases, but in maturity play is largely replaced by more businesslike concerns. Rhesus monkeys deprived throughout infancy of contact with agemates have difficulty joining a group as adolescents; they are socially awkward or overly aggressive. They have failed to learn the patterns and signals of the group and are unable to make or to interpret the intention movements charac-

teristic of its members. An important step in normal rhesus socialization is learning to play with peers.

THE BEGINNINGS OF SOCIAL PLAY IN CHILDREN

The young human, too, must learn to play with others like
himself. His earlier play with parents depended on their willingness to structure predictable sequences of sound, touch, and motion, and to carry much more than half the burden of communication. Other children differ from both adults and objects in being less controllable and less predictable. Although one young
child may find another very interesting, he does not quite know
what can be done with him. Observations of children in play
groups during the second year of life show that, when familiar
adults are present, children are attracted to their peers. They
spend a great deal of time watching each other's activities. There
are, however, somewhat conflicting findings concerning the
amount and type of social contacts that take place between ten
months and two years.

Several studies have put children together in a situation in
which their mothers were present but were instructed to talk
naturally with each other and not to initiate any interaction with
the toddlers. Carol Eckerman combined foursomes of same-age
toddlers and their mothers and assessed how much activity they
directed toward one another in a twenty-minute period (pairs
were aged ten months to a year, eighteen to twenty months, or
twenty-two months to two years).[7] Interaction between the children (as opposed to solitary activities or contacts with mother)
increased after twenty months, and it took the form of mutual
involvement with objects and direct involvement in one another's play: positive interaction (imitating or exchanging toys)
was more frequent than negative (struggling). Edward Mueller
observed a small play group of boys over several months and
found that the focus of activity gradually shifted from objects to
other children.[8] By eighteen months several children had learned
how to cooperate and take turns with a playmate in both complementary sequences (alternating leading and following) and in
imitative ones (reproducing the way another child handled an
object).

Wanda Bronson, however, reporting on a study still in progress, has observed very little change in how much infants initiate encounters with one another between ten months and two years, even though, like Mueller, she observed the same children over time.[9] Bronson's play groups were composed of three or four agemates (as was Mueller's single group) and, in all, forty children participated. She attributes the consistently low level of interaction between children of this age to their more compelling interest in the toys and objects in the room. Toddlers may be attracted to other toddlers, she suggests, but on investigation they find them too erratic to take many chances with. They snatch toys and are likely to cry or scream or poke at one. (About 45 percent of these children's brief encounters at each age ranged from mild to distressful disagreements or struggles.) The parent, it seems, remains the best person with whom to share toys and new sights and experiences. But Bronson did find qualitative changes in their behavior together. As the children became socially versatile, encounters became less transient, less tentative and "accidental." Disagreements did become more intense, though there were also more incidents involving cooperation or affection. These included offering objects, handling a toy together, and taking turns in brief bouts of Hide-and-Seek.

We can conclude that a two-year-old still has a great deal to learn about how to play with others. His social expertise rests on his experience with cooperative adults, and he must now learn how to sustain a mutually enjoyable encounter with a volatile and equally inept playmate. Human infants and infant primates (who unlike puppies and kittens are not normally reared in litters) do not appear to be able to interact with their peers before they are weaned, mobile, and able to use the communication systems unique to their species.

ROUGH-AND-TUMBLE PLAY

As they become more skilled in movement and communication, children become able to engage in what is called rough-and-tumble play. Rough and tumble is actually a shorthand term for a number of action patterns that are performed at a high pitch of activity, usually by a group. This type of play has been described by ethologists interested not only in play but in the total configuration of nursery-school activities. Typically, they observe a class or several classes over a period of time. Checklists of a variety of relatively simple, observable phenomena are prepared and defined as objectively as possible. The categories of these phenomena include facial expressions, vocalizations, postures and movements, aggressive behavior, other social gestures such as giving and showing. Items in the vocalization category, for example, usually include talk, scream, laugh, play noise, cry, sing. Other categories may specify the use of toys, equipment, and materials such as clay and paints. The age, sex, number of siblings, and length of nursery-school experience are usually noted for each child, and the time of day and the location (indoors or outdoors) may also be recorded. The raw data obtained are then analyzed first to determine how frequently the various items of behavior occur, what sorts of behavior cluster together in time, and then to relate these distributions of behavior to age, sex, school experience, and so forth.

From these accounts the cluster of activities called rough-and-tumble play has been identified. It is composed of run, hop, jump, fall over, chase, flee, wrestle, hit at, laugh, and make a face. It contrasts with aggressive conduct, which includes hit, push, take-tug-grab, stare down, and frown. Playfulness is signaled by laughter or making a play face, though exaggerated gestures or restraint in potentially violent movements probably also have communicative value. It is curious that there is so little information on the structure of children's rough-and-tumble play sequences as compared with the detailed accounts of cats and dogs provided by West, Bekoff, and others. We do not know how spontaneous bouts of chasing or mock fighting are conducted before organized and conventional playground games begin to appear. We do not know, for instance, what moves can start rough-and-tumble episodes, how longer sequences are built up, or how the bouts are usually concluded.

Studies conducted in England by Nicholas Blurton-Jones and by Peter Smith and Kevin Connolly provide the following picture of rough-and-tumble play at about four or five years of age.[10] It is more likely to occur out of doors and breaks out most spontaneously after children have just been released from a classroom or from set tasks. Compared with girls, boys engage in somewhat more vigorous activity with more noise and shouting and more close physical contact, such as wrestling and tumbling together. In a yard or designated play area, boys tend to move toward the periphery in larger mobile groups, and girls tend to play in a more restricted area, staying closer to the staff or playground equipment. Although girls also engage in rough and tumble, it is likely to be centered on slides or swings; and their groupings are smaller than those of boys.

In rough and tumble, as in other nursery-school activities, groups are usually made up of one sex. When other activities are taken into account, it appears that girls are attracted to more sedentary play with toys or art materials, tend to talk more with each other and spend more time with one or two partners. Boys race about more, make more and shorter social contacts, and focus less of their activity on toys and materials.

In general, younger children spend more time watching than engaging in boisterous play with others. Watching and observing may indeed be a form of exploration, and if so they would predictably precede spontaneous social play. However, even at about three years of age, children do take part in active social play, though they do so less often than older children. Their more cautious behavior may, in the groups observed, also reflect the fact that nursery school or other play group is a new experience for them. Observations of how new children are introduced and integrated into an existing nursery class show that it takes them some time to learn to interact with the more experienced children. For the neophytes, rough and tumble is the last activity they tend to engage in while getting acquainted with the veterans. It is also the case that first-born children spend more time watching and wandering about than do children with older siblings. These facts support the interpretation of rough and tumble as highly social and as different from intentional acts of aggression.

ROUGH AND TUMBLE IN OTHER CULTURES

The picture of rough and tumble in English and American nursery schools sketched above is probably widely valid. Boisterous, noisy, physical play in family, household, or village groups has been reported in diverse cultures, for example, among the Ilocano of Luzon, the Mixtecans of Mexico, and the Taira of Okinawa. It has been found that boys engage in more rowdy play than girls and that their groups move about more and further away from adults. But even such natural, spontaneous activities as chasing and rough-housing are shaped by culture and environment. Among the Pilaga Indians and the !Kung of Botswana, girls often engage in rough play. The !Kung boys and girls play together; the Pilaga do too, but often with the boys matched off against the girls. Pilaga girls from different villages conduct boxing bouts that appear violent, but in which actual injury is not sanctioned.

The nature of a young child's social experience is of course related to community and family organization and to the child-rearing practices of his society (for instance, time of weaning, treatment of a child after the birth of a sibling, and time at which responsibilities are assigned). In the non-Western and nonurban cultures mentioned above, children in late infancy or early childhood spend much of their time in the care of older siblings and often with other relatives or neighbors. If the households are isolated, the play groups are likely to be small, composed of mixed ages and both sexes; if the dwellings are close together and the community organization is open, then the groups are larger, but still include a range of ages. Toys—articles made especially for use by the young—are rare in all these communities and (with the exception of the Mixtecans, who discourage group play for girls) children are generally expected to play together. The Nydeggers wrote of the Ilocanos: "Just as adults are expected to want companionship so the assumption is made with children. A child playing alone must be lonely. The most striking thing about children's play is that it is almost never solitary. Play groups are encouraged if they are not voluntarily formed."[11] It seems that because of this attitude toward sociability, because each child is cared for by a number of others—some still children themselves—and because he is exposed early to many other boys and girls of various ages, active social play appears sooner in these societies than in English and American nursery schools, where many children encounter unfamiliar agemates for the first time.

In most cultures, play with motion for its own sake is joined with other aspects of play into more complex patterns. Rope jumping conjoined with rhymed verses; chasing and fleeing within a framework of social roles or themes such as Cops-and-Robbers; and group or team activities that have specified rules, limits, and sanctions, such as Hopscotch and Hide-and-Seek—all contain an action base of vigorous movement. In most human cultures play with motion does not disappear with approaching maturity, although it does come increasingly under the influence of social constraints and conventions that specify how, when, where, and by whom and in what garb the more boisterous and active types of play can be indulged.

4 / Play with Objects

Finding out what things are, how they work, and what to do with them occupies a great deal of the attention and efforts of the toddler and the young child. The term "toy" is often given to things that adults have designed or selected specifically to engage a child, but fascination with the properties of things extends to many other objects as well. It is perhaps this attractiveness of objects which has encouraged their widespread use as a research tool in the study of children's behavior, though they have an added advantage for the investigator in that they can be counted and their use described fairly objectively.

Objects serve as a link between the child and his environment in a number of ways. They provide a means by which a child can represent or express his feelings, concerns, or preoccupying interests. They also provide a channel for social interaction with adults or other children. Further, for the child an unfamiliar object tends to set up a chain of exploration, familiarization, and eventual understanding: an often-repeated sequence that will eventually lead to more mature conceptions of the properties (shape, texture, size) of the physical world.

Before examining play with objects, we can briefly review the immense achievements in the first year of life which make such play possible. Some of these accomplishments—the first step, the first word—are noted by parents. Other equally important achievements are seldom remarked, in part perhaps because they emerge gradually. For example, play with objects requires the achievement of visually directed grasping and adequate eye and hand coordination so that the child can pick up, hold, and turn objects. Such play further depends on the achievement of "object permanence," which is the understanding that an object continues to exist even though it is temporarily out of sight. It also requires some differentiation of action patterns, that is, the ability to perform different actions with an object. And building on the increasing voluntary control of physical movement, a baby develops the ability to repeat an action he has performed previously. More demanding still is the re-creation of an action someone else has performed—that is, imitation.

Imitation itself is a gradually emerging achievement that rests on both mental and physical development. The child first shows an ability to imitate certain actions he sees others perform; thereafter he will reproduce actions that he may have noticed several hours or even days before. This ability, called "delayed imitation," reflects the emerging capability to construct mental representations of actions and events, remember them, and be able to call them up even when the model is absent. At first this "memory" for actions is directly related to the physical sensations of performing the actions. At this time a child does not have verbal labels for action sequences or for objects, and his "concept" of an object is based on the sensory feedback of his experience with it. The object and his related action (patting a toy, opening a box) are therefore not separate phenomena. Jerome Bruner describes this mode of representing an action-object experience as the "enactive mode." Following this stage a child comes to make a distinction between the repeatable action pattern and the object or objects with which it was first linked. The nature of the child's representation of actions and their relations to objects next moves toward what Bruner has called the "iconic mode," the mode in which images or pictures of events and experiences organize the child's mental activities. Finally, as the child learns to associate the arbitrary and conventional labels of language with his own experiences, he moves into the "symbolic mode" of representation. He becomes able to symbolize an object or event with a word and gains yet another means for storing and retrieving aspects of his past experience. The symbolic mode of representation also enables him to use one object to represent another object. Thus the advent of symbolization ushers in the possibility of playing in a *qualitatively different way.*[1]

HOW OBJECT PLAY BEGINS

A composite picture of the changes that take place in a child's encounters with objects over the first three years can be drawn from the recent work of several psychologists. Although the procedures differed among the studies (for example, a child observed at home or a child seen in laboratory; limited sets of objects presented or a large group of objects presented), the trends toward more discriminating treatment of objects and greater complexity of object combinations are clear. In the following account, the ages are only approximate—individual children vary, some exhibiting a given type of behavior a bit earlier, some a bit later.

Several miniature objects—a cup, saucer, spoon, hairbrush, truck, trailer, doll—are placed before a child on a table. What is he likely to do? Following, in part, the work of Marianne Lowe,[2] we can predict that:

At *nine months*, the child will grasp a nearer, brighter object and bring it to his mouth; grasp another and do the same. After mouthing the object, he might well wave it or bang it on the table, then inspect it, turn it around, and bang it again or return it to his mouth. He uses only a few action patterns.

At *twelve months*, the child is likely to investigate (look at, turn, finger) each object *before* doing anything else with it. He might then put the spoon in his mouth once or twice, place it in the cup, and perhaps place the cup on the saucer, but other objects are still treated at random (mouthed, banged, waved).

At *fifteen months*, inspecting and investigating clearly precede other behavior. More and more consistently objects are accorded appropriate, or conventional, uses. The child will place the cup on the saucer and sip from it, and the spoon will be used more deliberately as if he were feeding himself. He will pick up the brush and run it over his hair; next he may push the truck back and forth. He may make the doll stand up.

At *twenty-one months*, the child will search for an object to "go with" other things. After putting the cup on the saucer, he will look for the spoon, find it, stir the imaginary drink and then drink it. He will then give the doll a drink from the cup or perhaps offer the observer a drink. He might brush his hair very carefully. He might place the doll in the truck.

At *twenty-four months*, the child feeds the doll realistically and lays it down for a nap after lunch. He brushes its hair and takes it for a ride in the truck. The truck and trailer will be lined up as if the truck were pulling the trailer, and the child may search for something to load into the trailer.

Between *thirty and thirty-six months*, the child will move the doll, making it pick up the cup and drink, then wash and dry the dishes, and put them away. The doll is made to brush its own hair. Thus the power to act purposefully is attributed to the doll. The truck and trailer are hooked together and moved with motor noises, and the doll may be made to drive the truck, perhaps to some specific location and back.

Over the two-year period these important developments stand out:

1. The child increasingly differentiates between various action patterns compatible with each object, and he fits together action and object appropriately (for example, he moves from mouthing every graspable object to putting only the spoon in his mouth).
2. He comes to combine objects that go together into functional relationships (he assembles the cup, saucer, and spoon).
3. He puts action patterns in sequence to form larger, coherent wholes (he links cooking, eating, and washing up).
4. He applies action patterns to himself (brushes his own hair), then to others or replicas of others (he brushes his mother's or a doll's hair). Finally, he attributes to replicas the ability to act (as when he causes the doll to brush its own hair or moves a toy dog while making barking noises).
5. He invents absent but appropriate objects or substances to complete action patterns (he stirs imaginary coffee with a toy spoon).
6. He transforms objects for use in actions and action sequences (he stirs imaginary coffee with a toy rake, used as a spoon).

These abilities are developed by acting on and interacting with the things and people around him. Their appearance through the second year of life indicates that the child is learning to play and beginning to engage in make-believe. But, more, these developments also reflect the beginnings of symbolic representation, a prerequisite to the development of language and abstract thinking. A progression from dependence on the physical properties of things to an ability to use signs that are completely arbitrary and conventional is well under way. The physical properties of things are taken as indications of their possible use, but they no longer solely determine that use. How exactly do these changes come about and how are they related? These are precisely the questions that are now being asked—and we still have no very full answers.

The manner in which the transformation of objects may develop has been suggested by Greta Fein of Princeton.[3] She presents a picture of orderly progression from single transformations to multiple ones. Fein tested forty-eight children between the ages of twenty-two and twenty-seven months to determine the conditions under which they would be able to use more and less realistic elements in a familiar action pattern; X eats from Y. These children were able to make a toy stuffed horse (X) eat from a plastic egg cup (Y). Most could also carry out the action with either a flat metal horse shape (X') and the egg cup (Y) or with the plush horse (X) and a shell (Y') for a food container. But when two substitutions were required at the same time (X' for X and Y' for Y, simultaneously), the children were not able to make the metal horse shape eat from the shell as if it were a dish or cup. Of course, even the toy horse and the egg cup, if they are combined in representing the action of eating, require transformation from a purely self-referenced experience of being fed or of feeding oneself. And to "feed the horse" one must treat the horse shape as if it were alive and the cup as if it contained food. But as the objects become more schematic, still further transformational steps are required. Fein's study suggests that learning to engage in symbolic play with objects progresses along a course from simple, single transformations to multiple and more complex ones. She concludes that in early make-believe activities an anchor (or realistic support) is required. Other studies have supported the notion that, when children first begin to play with objects, realistic replicas assist in their progress toward more imaginative deployment and combination of objects in pretend play. After a child has learned how to make believe, however, *less* realistic objects appear to facilitate make-believe play. They afford more scope for inventiveness and imagination, permitting the child to transform them to suit the occasion. Thus, for a skilled pretender, large cardboard boxes can be transformed into the family's home, the towers of a fort, a cave, cars on a freight train, or a witch's hut.

There is a paradox in the growth of pretending. As children become older, their use of objects in make-believe play becomes increasingly "appropriate." They represent more and more of the adult world in ways intelligible to us. The play becomes more realistic in that a greater range of details are provided, there are fewer idiosyncratic uses of objects and often greater faithfulness to the way things are in real life. At the same time, however, other details are treated quite cavalierly; there are often great flights of imagination and spur-of-the-moment invention. This paradox can be resolved in part when we look at a more advanced level of pretend play involving objects, a level typical of our three year old pairs. When a child is able to arrange utensils on a table, serve another child, tell him not to eat with his knife, and warn him that the food is very hot—all quite realistically—she may also appropriate the iron to serve as a teapot, if a proper one is missing. She will drastically abbreviate the time needed to cook a supper and will be quite happy to serve apple sauce from an empty pan. She may be oblivious to the fact that the dining table was, moments ago, the family car, or she may tell her partner to use a stuffed animal for a chair. Some aspects of this episode are only suggestive or schematic, as Lowe also observed in her subjects at three. It appears that the complex action plan, here the notion of serving and dining, has become more important than the objects themselves.

FROM DISCOVERY AND EXPLORATION TO EXPLOITATION AND PLAY

What happens when a young child encounters an object that is new to him? Will he begin straight away to play with it? Most usually he will not. There is, instead, a progression from discovery and simple manipulation to imaginative use of objects.

It is obviously not easy to cut up what may occur as a continuous flow of activity, but certain distinctions can be made according to the degree to which unrestrained and spontaneous play predominates. Listed in order of increasing adaptation to an object or experience are (a) exploration, (b) manipulation, (c) practice, and (d) repetition, with or without imaginative elaboration. Some of these terms have also been applied to aspects of play other than use of objects, but the following example will illustrate how these four types of orientation appeared in succession in one child's encounter with an object that was new to him. A three-year-old boy saw a large wooden car in our playroom for the first time. (a) He paused, inspected it, and touched it. (b) He then tried to find out what it could do. He turned the steering wheel, felt the license plate, looked for a horn, and tried to get on the car. (c) Having figured out what the object was and what it could do, he got to work on what *he* could do with *it*. He put telephones on it, took them off, next put cups and dishes on it. These activities were a form of trying out ideas to see how they would work. Finally, the car was understood, its properties and immediate usefulness reasonably clear. (d) He then climbed on it and drove furiously back and forth with suitable motor and horn noises. We can readily accept the last activity as play. The activities that led up to the last incident, however, seem less playful. Though (a), (b), and (c) do not seem quite like hard work, they do suggest a process of continuous testing and of learning what the object is and how it might be treated.

An important study by Corinne Hutt was designed specifically to disentangle the characteristics of exploration from those of play.[4] She constructed a novel object—a box with a movable lever to which four visible counters, a buzzer, and a bell were connected. Movements of the lever were recorded by the counters. Depending on how the object was preset, moving the lever could produce four different effects: (a) bell and buzzer sounding, counters visible; (b) bell and buzzer sounding, counters covered; (c) bell and buzzer off, counters visible; (d) bell and buzzer off, counters covered. Nursery-school children, aged three to five, were brought individually to a familiar room containing the box and five more conventional toys. Each child had six ten-minute sessions with the object. The children would approach it, inspect it, and then begin to manipulate the lever. They soon tired of the box when moving the lever produced no effects (d), and even with a view of the moving counters (c) their attention flagged by the third session. Producing noises with the bell and buzzer (b) kept them actively occupied through the fifth session. Addition of the visible counters to the sound effects, however, elicited the most extensive manipulation of the lever. The complexity of the results obtained from working the lever, and particularly the sound of bell and buzzer, promoted and increased active contact with the object.

Hutt also observed distinct differences between investigative-exploratory behavior and certain other types of behavior that were directed to the novel object. The former were characterized by full attention, facing and looking directly toward the object, cautiously feeling and touching it. The latter included many more diverse activities, which were actually of two types. One kind included repetitive movements (like patting the lever over and over again), continuous handling without looking at it directly (leaning on the lever to give a continuous ring while looking around the room), and subordinating the object to some other action plan (for instance, racing around the room carrying a truck and ringing the bell at each pass). The other kind Hutt called "transposition-function"; the child used the object for some other purpose (perhaps climbed on it, walked over it, or sat on it). The illustrations here very clearly show the contrasts between the concentration of exploration and the nonchalance and enjoyment of play.

The processes of exploration and familiarization, which must precede play with novel objects, new settings, unfamiliar events or unknown persons, are obviously associated with learning—that is, developing new conceptualizations for dealing with parts of the world. But perhaps play also contributes to learning in some way. Although the properties of an object (what it is, what it can do) may be known to some extent, new possibilities for its use or its potentiality for combination may be discovered in the course of playing with it. By definition, such learning would be "incidental" since the term "play" is restricted to activity that lacks any extrinsic goal. Still, the play orientation might conceivably facilitate what we would call creativity and what some psychologists have named divergent thinking.* The possibility that a playful orientation promotes insight into solutions of problems or that a playful orientation is characteristic of creativ-

*Divergent thinkers are good at flights of imagination, as in dreaming up the most, and also the most original, uses for a simple object. Convergent thinkers tend to arrive at more conventional solutions in an orderly way. We all use convergent and divergent thinking, though some people are more strongly disposed to one or the other style.

Characteristic patterns of exploring a novel object

ity has motivated a good deal of research. Obviously these possibilities have important implications for educational practices as well as for an understanding of how scientific discoveries and artistic innovations come about.

CREATIVE PROBLEM SOLVING AND OBJECT PLAY

It may now be clearer why a more precise distinction between exploration and play is important. What is the relationship between play and innovative or successful problem solving? Phrased more generally, does play promote creative thinking?

Kathy Sylva has attempted to distinguish between the effects of manipulating and becoming familiar with objects and the effects of prior playful, imaginative behavior involving the objects later used as tools in the solution of a task.[5] Sylva asked middle-class children from a day-care center to get a piece of chalk out of a plastic box that opened on release of a simple latch. The box was out of reach of hand and could not be touched by either of two sticks that were provided along with two clamps. The solution to the problem was to clamp the sticks together, flip up the latch with the extended stick, and rake the chalk out. Several different experimental conditions preceded the children's attempts at solution. In one experiment, some children watched an adult construct the tool; others were permitted to handle the tools freely and play with them if they liked. In another experiment some children watched an adult dramatize the construction of the tool by animating "Mr. Clamp," who put his teeth around the sticks. Still other children were given specific training in how to construct the tool. Regardless of their experience prior to the attempted solution, all children were given standardized hints if they did not proceed by themselves to the solution. The prior experience of freely handling the sticks and clamps was just as effective as watching an adult demonstrate the correct combination. Prior free handling, however, also led to more subsequent activity directed to the ultimate goal of obtaining the chalk; to somewhat more systematic, step-by-step procedures; and to more effective use of the hints, if hints had been given. Surprisingly, watching the amusing dramatization and receiving training were both relatively ineffective. Sylva concluded that free handling was more effective because only then did the children initiate the solution themselves. They had had the opportunity to explore alternative steps in the process and had also gained, perhaps, a more relaxed attitude toward the task.

But how do we know that the free handling was play? It could have been exploration or manipulation lacking any playful orientation to the objects. Sylva reexamined the behavior and success of those children who had the prior experience of handling the objects and found that a majority of them had actually played; they had engaged in some transformation of the materials, such as shaping a house or forming a letter A. The "transformers" were the children whose problem-solving performances were most efficient and effective. Thus, although it is not correct to say that playing *caused* better problem solving, it is true that those children who displayed nonliteral or imaginative behavior prior to the task were the best problem solvers.

THE ROLE OF OBJECTS IN SOCIAL CONTACTS

Objects are the prime currency of social exchange for the toddler. Through the second year of life, showing, sharing, giving, retrieving, and appropriating are the most frequent bases for his voluntary interactions with adults and other children. Newly mobile infants observed on a park outing with their mothers would quickly move away from the mother. When they encountered some arresting object, they would either turn to the mother and point to it while looking directly at her or, if the object was portable, bring it back for her inspection. In situations of more controlled observation children of twelve to eighteen months have been shown to bring or show adults (parent or observer) what they find interesting, and to do so often and continuously.

From twice-weekly observations of a play group of toddlers, Edward Mueller noted that virtually the only concerted action of the five otherwise independent members of the group followed on "discovery" of some object.[6] For example, when one child accidentally caused the bell of a train to ring, all the children gathered around the train to touch or try to ring the bell. A common focus of attention sustained an episode of parallel play. As Mueller put it, "The children did not interact with one another, so much as they unilaterally and simultaneously acted upon a common object." He found, however, that later in the three-month observation period two children's joint object-centered behavior sometimes changed into more person-centered interactions. Initially drawn to the train Loren was pulling, Robert began to follow Loren and then to imitate the course and direction of Loren's movements. At this point Loren became interested in Robert's running. Alternating rounds of lead and follow, with "happy-sounding cries and screams," grew out of Robert's initial pursuit of the object. Direct involvement with the same toy has been widely observed to be the most common basis for child-related behavior in groups of two-year-olds. Among somewhat older children, objects are still an important part of social exchanges. The Waterhouses in their study of English nursery classes observed that a newcomer to the class was first contacted with "gifts."[7] Toys, sweets, or personal belongings were offered in the overtures to friendship.

Showing a familiar object to a new adult or a new object to a familiar adult appears in itself to be one of the basic forms of communication for very young children. But the vocalizing that generally accompanies showing begins to stabilize to fairly consistent signals. One infant may use *Ha! Ha!*, another *Eee!* to accompany pointing, but each may use quite a different signal when giving. Most adults are responsive to these physical gestures, which are easily interpreted as sharing. The adults predictably respond with some type of recognition by looking, smiling, reaching, and often by saying *Thank you* or *Isn't that pretty?* Thus, not only does the object serve as a vehicle for communication, but sharing objects is one of the first events in which verbal communication becomes closely linked to a specific action performed by a child in a social situation.

Of course, objects have another, powerful attraction: they can be possessed. The short- or long-term association of person and object is one of the earliest concepts encoded in speech and appears in unambiguous form by the time the child can form two-word utterances. From that time at least, but probably even before speech, possession is an important notion. I was once introduced to a two-year-old and said, "Hello, Betsy. How are you?" "Mine," she responded firmly, holding out a coloring book.

A number of studies of nursery-school groups and of pairs of mothers and children in laboratory playrooms have implicated objects as the focus not only of cooperation and pleasant reciprocal exchanges but also of contention and physical struggle. Ownership or even temporary possession of an object by another child makes that object doubly interesting. Carol Eckerman noted that for two-year-olds "a toy on the ground does not equal a toy in the hand of a peer."[8] Contentions most usually involve a struggle over objects. Just taking or attempting to take an object from another child, however, is not necessarily an aggressive move on the part of a toddler. That is, such an action may not actually be "intended" as hurtful. Often the child who reaches out to appropriate another's toy is clearly taken aback and surprised when the owner howls or struggles.

Assignment of possession was a major focus of conversation between several pairs of three-year-olds in our paired agemate sessions. The discussions were usually pursued quite solemnly and harmoniously. One instance concerned a dress-up hat found in a box: A: *Is this yours?* B: *No.* A: *It's mine?* B: *Yes.* A: *It's mine?* B: *Sure it is.* Equitable distribution of objects for some other purpose was also an absorbing activity. Several pairs became so engrossed with apportioning props for a tea party that the party itself was forgotten: A: *You get a knife and I get a knife.* B: *Here's a cup for me and a cup for you.* A: *Where's my saucer?* B: *Here's a blue saucer for you and the green one is for me,* and so on and on until every item had been allocated.

Play with objects has important links with social development. Reflection on our own earliest childhood memories, however, may reveal that certain objects had strong private emotional appeal. Many people's earliest and most vivid recollections are of some toy. My own are of almost perfect tiny replicas of a table service complete with a fat, brown roast turkey on a platter, red cranberry sauce, vegetables, and a centerpiece of flowers, all part of the furnishings of a doll's house. The powerful emotional appeal of direct experience with objects is captured by the novelist John Updike, writing in *Women and Museums* of childhood visits to a museum where he was entranced by several small bronze figures: "They were in their smallness like secret thoughts of mine projected into dimension and permanence, and they returned to me as a response that carved strangely into parts of my body."

TOY PREFERENCES

The fact that children are attracted to certain kinds of toys along sex-appropriate lines is well known, and some psychologists have considered toy preference as indicative of the child's own sexual identification. Boys consistently choose "masculine" kinds of toys such as soldiers or trucks. Although girls tend to choose dolls and household objects, their interests are generally more versatile. Girls also choose masculine toys, though less consistently than boys do. The origins of these preferences can be traced in large part to parental behavior, to the parents' influence as models and to their approval or support of children's interest in sex-stereotyped objects. A very striking example of even more direct parental control of children's early exposure to types of toys is provided by a study of the private rooms of ninety-six children of upper-middle-class families, in age from under one to six.[9] There was no great difference between the boys' and girls' rooms in respect to the presence of books, furniture, musical objects, and stuffed animals. Boys had more varieties of objects than girls did. The boys' rooms contained far more toy animals in barns or zoos, objects relating to space, matter, energy, or time (magnets, puzzles, space ships). The girls' rooms contained more dolls, floral designs on wallpaper and fabrics, and ruffles or lace. Even though boys' rooms contained some dolls (for instance, cowboys), virtually none represented females or babies.

The most extreme difference was in the number of vehicles owned by the boys (375) as compared to the girls (17). No girl at any age had a wagon, bus, motorcycle, boat, or trailer. The typical boy of two had at least three vehicles and by the age of three the average was eleven. Further, only boys had live animals, depots, replicas of heavy equipment, and military toys; only girls had doll's houses, stoves, tea sets, and cradles for dolls. Harriet Rheingold, who directed this study, observes that in her laboratory girls of eighteen months spent as much time playing with trucks as boys did. She concludes that parents were not acceding to the spontaneous interests of their children but were themselves primarily responsible for the extremely different inventories of objects found in the boys' and girls' private rooms. The high-level socioeconomic class in this study might be expected to be less extreme in regard to sex stereotyping than the general population, so that this difference in the toys given to boys and girls is probably quite widespread. Certainly the sex preferences in toys in freely chosen activities in nursery schools, which Margaret Parten remarked on in 1933, are still in evidence today.[10] Boys cluster at the tool bench or push trucks around the room, and girls gather in the kitchen corner to cook and wash dishes in most of the free-activity periods we have observed.

EXPRESSIVE BEHAVIOR WITH OBJECTS

In their play with dolls and other objects children sometimes appear to associate the dolls with members of their own families and will almost always choose a same-sex doll to represent themselves. Children may portray events they themselves have experienced and represent situations that presumably have some importance for them. Objects are thus incorporated into the child's expressive behavior. These expressive aspects have led to clinical and therapeutic applications of the child's treatment of dolls and other toys. I will not go into play therapy except to note that therapists generally stress its cathartic aspects. They stress the notion that, by representing a traumatic experience or situation symbolically and by returning to it and perhaps reversing its outcome in play, the child becomes better able to deal with the problem in his real life. One of the values of play for therapy has been stated by Erik Erikson: "That the metaphoric expression of intimate experiences in free play 'loosens' the communicability of these same experiences is, of course, the main rationale of play therapy."[11]

Doll play with a restricted inventory of realistically constructed human figures has been widely used to study aggression, racial prejudice, parent preference, and attitudes toward siblings. Anthropologists Jules and Zunia Henry employed a typical procedure to study sibling rivalry among Pilaga Indian children in Argentina.[12] These children are abruptly displaced at the birth of a sibling and ignored by parents and relatives, who turn all their attention to the new infant. The rejected children were given realistic dolls matched in sex, age, and number to members of their own family. Though unaccustomed to realistic dolls (their own were crudely formed of bone and clay), the children played with the new dolls in their normal fashion, representing familiar but impersonal and stereotyped village and family activities. When the Henrys named the new dolls for the children and members of their family, however, the play became more personal. The children manipulated the self-doll and the others to symbolize hostility (kicking and biting). The dramatized aggression was directed at parents and siblings, and even toward themselves. The children also depicted the self-doll as nursing, which the Henrys interpreted as indicating a desire to return to their former, more favored status as infants.

Caution is necessary in drawing inferences about a child's attitudes, emotions, or previous experiences from his choice or treatment of objects. Two qualifications must be taken into account. First, even a child is aware that there is an important difference between depicting an event through objects or props and actually experiencing that event. It is true that at times the child appears to forget these facts when he is playing, but play generally reflects a *willing* suspension of disbelief. Second, treatment of objects in play is not actually realistic. Although some behavior is copied faithfully from a model, some is only roughly suggestive of events in the nonplay world. The child does select those aspects of experience that matter most to him, but there is also an element of convention or stylization in the depictions of his experience. Further, the child can combine both remembered and imagined events, mixing into one sequence material from a bedtime story, memories of actual events, an image from a television program, a frustrated impulse, a scene witnessed in another child's home, and a stereotyped association of objects and people or of objects and acts that he has learned in a previous play episode with friends.

If these cautions are kept in mind, then children's attraction to objects and replicas and their willingness and ability to depict events by manipulating toys can be used to learn from the child what he is not able to convey directly or succinctly in conversations or interviews with an adult. Although I will discuss this topic more extensively in Chapter Six, it is appropriate here to describe briefly a very interesting use of object play as a research technique. Sidney Brower and some associates are designing play spaces for children in lower socioeconomic neighborhoods in a crowded urban area in the United States. They have brought together pairs of elementary-school classmates, including some aged six, and have presented them with a schematic, scaled-down model of a typical area with streets, alleys, sidewalks, houses, and small backyards. The children are given a few cars and several parent and child dolls. The behavior that results (with very little prompting and only a few suggestions, such as *Show us your favorite games*) is videotaped. Amazingly fluent representations of sidewalk and street games, car accidents and their consequences, and other important and exciting events have been obtained. The parent dolls warn against the dangers of the street; a game of Dodge Ball or Hide-and-Seek is conducted in great detail; a group of boys ventures into another neighborhood and is chased off by bigger boys and their dogs. There are dramatic exaggerations and elements of fantasy, but certain themes and incidents recur among different pairs of children. Gradually a composite picture of the patterns of activities and use of spaces characteristic of these children emerges; and this picture can be checked with first-hand observations and with interviews and reports as well. This information can then be used in designing play spaces compatible with the needs and interests of the children and the neighborhoods.

Throughout childhood, play with objects undergoes many changes. As the child becomes more skilled and experienced, his playful treatment of objects becomes more diverse and sophisticated. Both imagination and intellectual curiosity begin to contribute to his play—paper dolls are clad in colorful and detailed costumes; intricate constructions are built from modeling sets or sand. More and more, meaningful associations accrue to objects, and play with objects is combined with other aspects of play. Often, as we will see in later chapters, objects are incorporated as props in dramatic play, or their treatment is governed by complex rules in games of physical or intellectual skill. All through these changes, however, objects continue to arouse curiosity and the desire to learn. They provide enjoyment in mastering their use or in understanding the properties of things, and they also continue to facilitate social contacts and to assist in the expression of ideas and feelings.

5 / Play with Language

The use of newly acquired resources for playful exploitation is most striking in children's play with language. Almost all the levels of organization of language (phonology, grammar, meaning) and most phenomena of speech and talking, such as expressive noises, variation in timing and intensity, the distribution of talk between participants, the objectives of speech (what we try to accomplish by speaking) are potential resources for play. It is curious that there has been little systematic study of this topic, since play with language and speech provides overt and easily observable forms of behavior. But this behavior is rather difficult to quantify (a score of one for a pun? two for a rhyme?), and it is of course difficult to elicit in experimental studies. There are, however, a few excellent collections based on anecdotes or informal observations, and these suggest that the child from two to six is fascinated with the resources of language and that he is sensitive to the play potential in this newly discovered world.

The Russian writer of verses and stories for children, Kornei Chukovsky, sees in this period a time of verbal creativity when the newcomer to the world of linguistic sounds and symbols brings a fresh eye to the marvels of language.[1] Unlike the adult who is sated with the sounds and metaphoric nature of everyday language, the child finds word shapes and the figurative properties of meaning a source of delight. Chukovsky quotes a four-year-old who raced to the table with the original demand: *Give me, give me, before I die, lots and lots of potato pie.* Children's questions often reveal surprising insight into the meaning structure of language, as these queries indicate: Couldn't table legs be fitted with shoes? Since there is running water, is there sitting water? Did the man really leave town under a cloud? It is important to note that at least some of the child's "errors" in building new words are often a result of productive linguistic rules for word formation. He can create verbs from nouns—*I am blocking* (building a tower with blocks)—and he can create nouns from verbs—*Look! A sweep!* (on discovering a toy broom).

Extensive collections of jump-rope rhymes and songs, charms and chants, jokes and other verbal accompaniments to play activities have also been made, most notably by Iona and Peter Opie.[2] Other collections confirm their findings of a powerful and long-standing oral tradition of play with language in the folk cultures of school-age children. The Opies stress the historical and geographic continuity of form and function of these materials and suggest a direct transmission from child to child rather than adult-mediated diffusion. The reader probably remembers, for example, if he ever learned Pig Latin, that his instructor was not a parent but another child.

In this chapter we will be primarily concerned not with codified songs and rhymes or with traditional incantations, verbal jokes, and insults (*See my thumb? Boy, you're dumb!*) but with the more ephemeral productions of play with language. We will examine the unrehearsed use of linguistic resources for fun, first looking at verbal play with noises and sounds, then at the different linguistic levels of phonology, grammatical forms, and meaning, and finally at play with the pragmatic or functional aspects of conversation.

In our agemate sessions most of the play with language or speech was spontaneously generated rather than quoted. An exception was a fragment of a nursery rhyme produced as a descriptive comment. A girl of five saw that a doll was missing a shoe and ran off the lines, *One shoe off and one shoe on. Diddle diddle dumpkin my son John.* She and her partner smiled at this apt quotation, but no further play resulted. Of the few cases in which lines from traditional verses or tunes were repeated, most were solitary performances and only rarely did they become a basis for a joint production. We do not know why the songs and rhymes of nursery school and home were so rarely reflected in these sessions, but it is noteworthy that very little play was based directly on nursery school experiences such as games or class expeditions.

PLAY WITH NOISES AND SOUNDS

The most primitive level at which verbal play is conducted is that of articulation or phonation—the actual process of making sounds. In the babbling stage, usually at its peak between six and ten months, the child produces a great variety of sounds. These random noises, however, are not the immediate precursors of the vowels and consonants of language. Many disappear from the repertoire altogether, and others have little resemblance to the units of the phonological system which are later represented in the meaningful words of the language. Vocalizing does continue through the early periods of language acquisition but tends to appear only in noncommunicative settings. Recordings of solitary one-year-olds show long episodes of vocal modulation of a single vowel, with the voice melodically rising and falling, varied with other sound effects such as a quavering voice. Stable syllabic forms are also repeated at great length (for example, *Ba, Ba, Ba*), with or without minor vowel or consonant modifications. When the child does begin to talk (the first intelligible word is usually reported at about ten months to a year) and learns to produce and control the contrast between making vocal noises and speaking, it is then possible to identify episodes of verbal play with sound.

Repetitive, rhythmic vocalizations are associated with pleasurable states in the prelinguistic child, and infant-parent games very often include a vocal component. The parent's "swelling" oooh-sound of mock threats and loomings, the popping noises and tongue clicking that accompany tickling, finger-walking, or jiggling, are among the first models of vocal play the infant encounters. His own use of playful vocalizations continues as he learns to talk and, through the preschool period, becomes increasingly differentiated from other uses of speaking.

Syllable shapes and prosodic features such as intonation and stress provide the raw material for early language play. Controlled variation in articulation, such as rasping, whispering, or nasalization, are also favorite materials. Making noises can be enjoyed as absorbing in itself or can be used to provide special sound effects (such as engine noises). With strict regulation of tempo, vocal noises can provide rhythmic accompaniment for play with motion (humming or tongue clicking while hopping or banging some object).

Vocalizations as accompaniments to movement grow from hums, squeals, and bellowings to repetitive, often melodic strings of syllables. Music to iron a fish by was provided by a boy of three. The syllables *dá: ti, dá: ti** initiated the chant and were gradually varied in a loose singsong rhythm. Vowels provided the main source of variation. The sequence was:

Da ti di
da ti di
da ti di
da da da
do di da
do di da
di do da di go bo di
di do da di go bo di
di do da di go bo di

The boy's partner did not join in this chant.

Sequences of nonsense syllables move to chants built on recognizable word shapes with fairly regular patterns of stress and pitch. But in all these types of playful vocalization the meaning of the words is secondary or nonexistent, and it is only the sound and rhythm that are enjoyed or that enhance the accompanying activity. Harriet Johnson provides an example of a chant produced by a two-and-a-half-year-old upon completing a block-building project.[3]

Now it's dóne un ún
Dóne un ún un ún

Between the ages of two and three an important advance takes place. Conventionalized noises are learned and used to identify certain events and actions. These noises, each of which has a specific meaning, appear to be an almost essential part of the particular event or action. Moreover, insofar as they are conventional, the noises can also identify the meaning of what is

---

*A colon after a vowel symbol indicates lengthening. When it is pertinent to the discussion, relative stress, or loudness, is marked *directly over* a vowel by ´(primary stress and ` (secondary stress); unstressed syllables are unmarked.

happening for a playmate. Some of these noises are built from the sound units (phonemes) of the child's language, but others represent noises that do not occur in the formation of English words.

Examples of such action-identifying tags used by American children are: ding-a-ling (telephone), ruff-ruff (dog barking), tyap-tyap or nyam-nyam (sound of eating), pow-pow (explosions of a gun). Beep-beep is an automobile horn, and the racing-engine sound could be written as vroom-vroom, though that sound is much more complex than the spelling suggests.* Exact repetition of a syllable is the characteristic means of formation for most of the tags. They are used to fill in or elaborate the context of pretending and always accompany the appropriate physical activity.

Distortion of normal articulation over a whole utterance is another way in which vocal capabilities can be played with. Several pairs in our group engaged in "talking funny." For example, trying to speak with the lips held spread wide and rigid or talking in a squeaky or gruff voice was a source of amusement in itself and could be shared by both. Just talking funny is somewhat different from changing the voice to signal an adopted identity, such as infant, father, baby fish, in episodes of make-believe with role enactment (see Chapter Eight). In the latter cases various aspects of speaking are used to mark an assumed role and to express pretend attitudes, but are not themselves the major focus of play.

Solitary singing or humming can be related thematically to some concurrent action, as was the chant *Now it's done un un*. But the song or chant can itself become a primary focus of attention, continuing beyond the action that triggered it off. For example, a boy (2:10) picked up a toy dunebuggy (named for him by one of the observers, who then left the room). First the word *dunebuggy* was explored for its syllabic possibilities, and the stress pattern was adjusted (*dúnebùggy → dúne bú-ggý*); next

---

*It is interesting that some of these forms involve sounds that do not occur in the phonological system employed in normal speech. *Vroom-vroom*, for example, uses a type of r-sound that is not a component of English phonology. Such sounds prove very difficult for adults attempting to learn foreign languages that do systematically employ the sounds.

the initial consonant was modified (*dune* → *june*) and the first syllable duplicated (*júne júne bú-ggý*); finally to the four approximately equally stressed syllables was added a rhythmic contour with slight terminal pitch rise. Throughout the three-minute sequence, the child walked about and casually examined a large wooden car and a stool with a magnifying glass in the center. The chant itself had become the focal activity while the object that triggered it was quite forgotten.

The preceding example utilizes sound for play, but the sounds are more clearly linguistic elements and the intonational features are similar if not identical to the prosodic features of pitch and stress that are part of the phonological system of communicative speech. Thus this example appears to be transitional between play with noises and sound and play with features of the linguistic system.

Playing with sounds and noises appears to be primarily a private activity. Only one report of social play with nonsense syllables has been published so far. Elinor Keenan videotaped her twins (2:10) during the first hours of a morning when they were alone.[4] She obtained a wide variety of joint, well-synchronized linguistic play activities (songs, poems, ritual insults) as well as instances of sound play, which she defined as "utterances which cannot be referentially interpreted by an adult native speaker." Some of these employed possible English syllables, but many included sounds or processes that are not part of the English phonological system. Since our pair sessions contained no such joint performances, it may be that only children who are very well acquainted can produce structured verbal play as in this excerpt from Keenan's twins:

Child 1	Child 2
(1) apshi: autshi: apshi: autshi: o:tshi: o:shabatsh	
	(2) sha: shabatsh:
(3) sho:babatsh	
	(4) sho:babat shobabatsh (laugh)
(5) sho:bababatsh	

PLAY WITH THE LINGUISTIC SYSTEM

The period from two to three is one of rapid linguistic achievement. Playful use of language at this time has been reported, though primarily for solitary children. The most detailed account is that by Ruth Weir, who recorded the presleep monologues of her son Anthony (2:10).[5] These recordings revealed the seemingly indefatigable practice of linguistic structures. Anthony experimented with the phonological properties of nonsense syllables and words: *Let Bobo bink. Bink ben bink. Blue kink.* He systematically substituted words of the same grammatical categories: *What color mop. What color glass.* He built up and broke down sentences, thus isolating their components: *Stop it. Stop the ball,* and *Anthony jump out again. Anthony jump.* He exercised conversational exchanges, often asking and answering questions, congratulating or warning himself, and he practiced counting, listing, and naming. His paragraphs, defined by Weir as sequences of utterances chained by phonological, grammatical, or semantic links, often show the simultaneous use of these links:

Anthony's speech	*Weir's comments*
That's office. That's office.	Sound play with the
Look Sophie.	pronunciation of *That's office*
That Sophie.	and *Sophie,* with substitution
Come last night.	in the sentence frame. Break-
Good boy.	ing down a complete sentence.
Go for glasses.	Recall of recent event and
Go for them.	self-congratulations on keeping
Go to the top.	hands off forbidden glasses.
Go throw . . . etc.	More systematic substitution in
	frame. Rhyming phrase.

It is likely that many children, when they are alone, conduct similar bouts of playful language exploration, which has been called practice play. In the reported cases of solitary monologuing the speech differs in a number of ways from the child's speech produced in conversations with a goal, as when he wishes to influence another person's actions. In private linguistic excursions the child becomes aware of the structural properties of his language and increasingly skilled in the fluent production of normal speech. He experiments with the componential structure of sentences as well as with their prosodic possibilities. In fact, he playfully takes apart and puts together building blocks of sequences that he cannot until several years later consciously isolate or decompose. Even at the beginning of elementary school, children cannot segment a word into syllables or identify the word boundaries in utterances when asked to do so. There is evidence, however, that children vary considerably in the degree to which they engage in such solitary practice with their newly acquired linguistic abilities, and we do not yet know whether practice play with language is essential to normal language development.

In social interactions among children, the distinction between such exploration of linguistic structure and play with language is somewhat clearer. First, each partner must know whether what the other has said requires a playful or nonplayful response, and thus the productions are distinctly marked as playful, if they are so intended. Second, the pressures of responsive communication do not permit the lengthy and leisurely unfolding of private meaning associations or privately intriguing sound variations, such as those Anthony pursued. Keenan's twins at 2:10 years did jointly produce, in alternating turns, sequences of nonsense syllables as well as intelligible phrases with rhymes and phonological variations that were very similar to Anthony's linguistic exercises. But in our pairs of acquainted and unacquainted children, play with language resources was rarely shared with a partner until after three. And then the interactive play with language tended to be repetitive and predictably structured—that is, less like a stream of associations and more like a measured, alternating current. However, from about three and a half virtually all levels of language structure were used as a basis for social play.

From this point on, we will examine social play with language as conducted in the pair sessions. In that setting, of course, the children could be socially engaged or could ignore one another altogether. When not engaged, one or both children sometimes produced private speech that was somewhat similar to Anthony's solitary performances; one example is the manipulation of the word *dunebuggy*. They made up chants and explored word shapes, but indulged in few grammatical buildups, breakdowns, and substitutions. One girl (3:4) in an unacquainted pair tried to engage her partner in a conversation. Failing to get a response she conducted a dialogue herself with an imaginary Mr. Smugla, which began:

Smugla, Mr. Smugla I can't bring my daughter.
Why? Why? Why? Why?
She didn't have any dresses—or shirts or pants.
Then I'll keep her in her pyjamas.
But she can't stay in them.

This continued for four minutes.

It may be that the very presence of another child, no matter how uncooperative, leads another child toward forms of language play that are less "analytical" and more like normal conversation.

SOCIAL PLAY

We can distinguish three types of social play with language: spontaneous rhyming and word play; play with fantasy and nonsense; and play with speech acts and discourse conventions. More than one type can be represented in a single interactive episode, but it appears that the distinctions have to do with some basically different uses of language resources for play.

Spontaneous rhyming and word play. Spontaneous social word play arose in our pair sessions from interactions already in progress, most commonly from states of mutual attending and desultory conversation. It did not tend to arise in more mutually absorbing states such as pretending or in goal-oriented episodes such as trying to fix a broken toy or arguing about something.

The most obvious type of word play is rhyme. Children's predilection for rhythm, rhyme, and alliteration is well known. Only a few simple rhymes were constructed by our sample of children. In the following instance, one child was responsible for the rhyme *high/sky;* the other repeated the leader's words and rhythm but concluded the sequence with a sincere request for information.

Boy (4:1)	*Boy (3:9)*
(handles small ladder and pipe)	(watches)
(1) I need ˋthis.	
	(2) You need ˋthat.
(3) You go ´way upˋ high.	
	(4) You go ´way upˋ high.
(5) You go ´high in theˋ sky. Nobody can ˌsee.	
	(6) Nobody can ´see?
	(7) Nobody can ´see?
(8) ˌYeah.	

A single word utterance provided a rhyming exchange for another pair: *sparky/darky*. However, only an older, previously acquainted pair produced a multiple exchange containing a sequence of rhymes and variations on word shape and prosodic features.

Boy (5:2)	*Girl (5:4)*

(both children simultaneously wander and handle various objects, little direct gaze)

(1) And when Melanie and . . . and you will be in here you have to be ˋgrandˋmother ´grand ˌmother. ´Right?*	
	(2) I'll have to be ˌgrand ´momma ˌgrandˌ momma ˋgrandˌ momma. (in distorted voice)
(3) ˌGrand⌢mother grand ⌢ mother ˌgrand ˌmother.	
	(4) ˌGrand⌢momma ˌgrand ˌmomma ˌgrand ˌmomma.
(5) ˌGrand⌢mother ˌgrand ˌmother ˌgrand ˌmother.	
	(6) ˌGrand⌢momma ˌgrand ˌmother ˌgrand ˌmomma.
(7) ˌMomma.	
	(8) ⌢Momma´I . . . . my ˌmommy ˌmomma.

*For a reminder about pitch markings, see the note on page 13.

(9) ˌMother ˌhumpf.

(10) ˋHey.

(11) ˋMother ˋmear (laugh)
ˋmother ˋsmear.

(laugh)

(12) I said ˋmother ˋsmear
ˌmother ˌnear ˌmother ˌtear
ˋmother ˋdear. (laugh)

(13) ˋPeer.

(14) ˋFear.

(15) ˌPooper.

(16) ´What?

(17) ˌPooper. Now ˋthat's a . . .
ˋthat's a good ˌname.

The stress and pitch possibilities and the common lexical variations (*mother, momma, mommy*) were fairly well exhausted by
this pair.

The sounds of words appear to be more available for spontaneous play than their grammatical shape. A common process
for forming diminutives is the addition of /i:/, spelled *y* or *ie*, to
the last consonant of a monosyllable (*doggie*) or to a nonfinal
consonant of a polysyllabic word (*Kathy* or *Robbie*). A formally
similar process changes a noun to an adjective that means "having the quality of the noun" (*fishy, rainy*). These were the only
grammatical operations the children played with. The first process, along with duplication of the word, is illustrated by the following exchange (all the words relate to toys and objects in our
observation room):

Boy (5:2)

(inspects stuffed animals)
(1) ˋTeddy bear's⌢mine.

(3) No, the ˋsnakey⌢snakey is
ˌyours.

Girl (5:7)

(busy with suitcase)

(2) The ˋfishy´fishy is⌢mine.

The adjective-forming process was used as the basis for a sophisticated exchange of pure word play:

Boy (5:7)	Girl (5:2)
(wandering)	(moving ironing board)
(1) 'Cause it's fishy too.	
(2) 'Cause it has fishes.	
	(3) And it's snakey too 'cause it has snakes and it's beary too because it has bears.
(4) And it's . . . and it's hatty 'cause it has hats.	

Play with fantasy and nonsense. Nonsense and verse, with or without rhyme, and nonsense stories add a dimension of meaning or meaning distortion as a resource for play. Nonsense verse and topsy-turvy meanings appeal to children of our age range. Chukovsky wrote, "Hardly has the child comprehended with certainty which objects go together and which do not, when he begins to listen happily to verses of absurdity."[6] And as soon as a child has learned how something is supposed to be, then it becomes a source of fun to distort it or exaggerate it in some way. The most productive process for making nonsense at the word level among our pairs was the creation of meaningless common nouns and of proper names that are odd or far-fetched.

Assignment of funny names to self, to partner, or to imaginary others reflects awareness of the importance of the normal name and address system. In nonplay exchanges, children are very insistent that they be called by their correct names. Several of them engaged in serious discussions on the choice or the correct pronunciation of their proper names. One girl objected to being called Karen and repeatedly pointed out that her mother called her Kiren.

There may be certain properties that make some types of play names especially amusing. Nonsense syllables, like *dingba*, *poopaw*; nonname words, like *Mrs. Fool-Around*; terms with scatological overtones, like *Uncle Poop*; and terms that are potentially insulting but that may also be used of self, like *Silly-face* or *Dumbhead*, served as themes for social play among all groups except the youngest. The following example represents at least two types:

Girl (5:7)   *Girl (5:1)*

(both children are using telephones to call friends)
(1) Mommy, mommy, I got
    new friends called Dool,
    Sol, Ta.

                                          (2) Dool, Sue, and ⌢Ta?

          (both laugh)
(3) Those are funny names,
    aren't they?

                                            (4) No, it's Poopoo, Daigi,
    and Dia . . . Diarrhea.

          (both laugh)

The manipulation of sense and nonsense is one of the components of many successful rhymes and stories written by adults for children, but children also create nonsense. They use outrageous names, juxtapose improbable elements, invent unlikely events, retaining just enough sense of the real world to hold the fabrication together. In several cases the nonsense is produced as if it were serious sense and *marked as play only by laughter after the performance.* With gestures and dramatic delivery, and a straight face, one boy (3:5) told another a story about his Thanksgiving turkey, which was caught, patched up with a bandaid, and cooked. It thereupon flew out the window. Both giggled happily after the narrative.

A girl pretended to write a letter with real paper and pencil. She produced the following poetic nonsense—which must have been her own unique creation and which was heartily appreciated by her partner:

Girl (4:9)   *Girl (4:7)*

(on the car, writing letter)   (listening and drumming on stove)
(1) Dear Uncle Poop, I would
    like you to give me a
    roasted meatball, some
    chicken pox . . .
(2) and some tools. Signed . . .
(3) Mrs. Fingernail. (smiles
    and looks up at partner)

                                                            (continued)

(4) Toop poop. (laughs)
Hey, are you Mrs. Finger-
nail?

(5) Yes, I'm Mrs. Fingernail.
(in grand, dignified voice)

(6) Poop, Mrs. Fingernail.
(giggles)

Manipulation of sense is often, except in intent, closely related to outright prevarication, and we must presume that when a child misnames or asserts an obvious untruth and marks it as playful, that he has some awareness of the distinction between truth and falsehood. But several factors are involved here, factors having to do with conversational usage.

Play with conversation. Conversation is built on a number of conventions that are actually guidelines for social transactions. Conversing is a highly cooperative venture, even when the tone is truculent or contentious. Linguists, sociologists, and philosophers have only relatively recently begun to study the assumptions about procedures, mutual expectations about content and sequence, and rules for regulating or engineering exchanges that speakers bring to particular speech situations. As a child learns to converse, he acquires these assumptions, expectations, and procedural rules—though even as an adult he may never be able to explicate them in a general fashion. Furthermore, the child learns most of what he knows about the rules for conversing not from explicit instruction but through first-hand experience of interacting with others in a variety of situations. Some "higher-level" guidelines may be verbalized by adults: *You must always tell the truth* or *When I ask you a question, answer me*—but such admonitions are generally addressed to children who already know quite well that truth is expected and that questions require replies.

To return to the topic of "truth," it is important to note that false assertions not only represent mismatches between words and certain events, but they also violate assumptions and expectations that make social interactions possible. One vital rule on which society depends is *Say what you believe to be true* (and not less and not more) or in more familiar words—*the truth, the whole truth, and nothing but the truth.* Play with false assertions is possible only if this social convention is well understood.

Anne Davison at the University of British Columbia has observed the beginnings of play with this discourse convention in two siblings, Sophie (3:2) and Jean (2:0).[7] A still younger child (1:10) did not apparently recognize what Davison calls nonserious speech, but Sophie found misnaming things and pictures in books quite funny—if the interlocutor was her mother. With an unfamiliar adult, however, she was less sure of the humorous intent and was uncertain how to respond. Jean also succeeded in playing with the convention with his mother, though he was easily recalled to seriousness if his mother did not go along with the joke.

Our agemates often broke this truth or sincerity rule with the apparent intent of creating a joke. A boy (5:2) asked a girl (5:5) whom she would rather be with—Mary Ann or Lisa. She looked at him quite soberly and replied *Um. I think . . . um . . . Lisa, because she's a boy.* The she giggled and her partner laughed and said *No, she's a gi::rl. You silly.* Asserting what is not, was not, or probably will not be can serve as a basis for social play only if both partners are aware that the orientation is playful. If that condition fails, then a false statement will be interpreted as deceit or error, not as play.

Children do play with conversational conventions even before they are able to conduct what adults would consider a coherent and "sensible" dialogue. However, the conventions that children can use in a nonplay manner they can also put to playful use. One convention that is quite productive of play can be stated roughly as: If an assertion has been made, and if you must contradict it, provide some support or justification for your contradiction or apologize for countering the assertion. Further, if the person who makes the assertion must reassert his position after being countered, he too must add some support. An example of the near-normal and nonplay use of this convention is:

Girl (2:10)	*Boy* (3:0)
(they hear a noise outside the room)	
(1) It might be your mommy.	
	(2) No. She's not coming.
(3) She's coming.	
	(4) No, she's not going down to pick me up. Joan is.

The same couple produced a playful episode based on violation of the same convention (as did almost all pairs):

Girl (2:10)	Boy (3:0)
(1) That's your cowboy hat when you go outside.	
	(2) No, no it's not.
(3) I bet it is.	
	(4) No it's not.
(5) Yes it is.	
	(6) No it's not.
(7) Yes it is.	
	(8) No.

A second convention that is both productive and popular for playful distortion is one that builds on what has been called an invitation question. The convention, however, is probably not restricted to questions. In adult conversation it operates somewhat as follows: Respond to a question or assertion concerning your own state or experience as an invitation to contribute to the conversation. Thus, if a conversational partner says to you *I heard that you had an unusual vacation,* a simple *yes* or *no* does not suffice to maintain interaction. As addressee, you have been invited to expand on the topic, for instance, *Yes, we spent a week in Portugal.* Some such convention appears to underlie our agemates' play episodes in which one partner repeatedly questions and the other answers but steadfastly refuses to elaborate. The absence of elaboration is particularly noticeable following a negative response:

Girl (3:7)	Boy (3:7)
	(has just put on fireman's hat)
(1) Is that your fire hat?	
	(2) Yeah.
(3) Did you get it from school?	
	(4) Nope.
(5) From here?	
	(6) Nope.

(7) Where? In the car?

     (8) Um, no.

(9) From you?

     (10) No.

(11) From in the . . . the
other room?

     (12) No. Yes.

A nonplay or literal use of the same convention is, as might be predicted, also possible for this same pair: A: *You changed your mind?* B: *Yes, I want to be the daddy.*

When people talk to each other, they not only convey facts or reveal emotions; they perform meaningful social acts. They warn, promise, command, ask permission. These essential, interpersonal events have been called speech acts. The English philosopher John Austin pointed out that certain formulations do not refer to social acts but are in fact themselves social acts—for instance, an apology is accomplished by saying *I apologize*; one enters into the contract we term "promising" by saying *I promise.*[8] Underlying the successful performance and interpretation of such acts are the shared understandings of the speakers. A successful request for information (a question) rests on the beliefs that the speaker does not already know the answer, that he wishes to know the answer, and that he believes the addressee is able and willing to divulge the answer but is not going to do so without the impetus of the request. Our pairs played with requests for information most often by violating the underlying belief conditions that the speaker did not already know the answer and that he wanted the requested information. In the following example, the pair enjoyed a series of pointless questions and obvious answers:

Boy (5:2)

(picks up dress-up items)
(1) What is this?

(3) What is this?

Girl (5:7)

(sits on car)

  (2) It's a party hat.

  (4) Hat.

        (continued)

(5) Funny. And what is
this?

(6) Dress.

(7) Yuck.

(8) And what is this?

(9) Tie.

(10) All yucky stuff.

Speech, of course, enters into the other aspects of play as a marker of playful orientation, as a means of managing the complex activities of make-believe, and as a component in the expressive behavior of pretending. As we shall see later, much ritualized play is also built on the resources provided by language and speech.

From the vocalizations built on syllable structures to the relatively sophisticated violations of the structure of speech acts or of conversational conventions, almost every type of systematic regularity of language form and use is available for play. The more we understand of the various facets of language use, the better we will be able to identify instances of children's play with the resources of language and communication.

6 / Play with Social Materials

In all the aspects of play, four developmental trends are evident. First there are, obviously, processes of biological maturation, of increasing skill and competence with respect to the varied facets of experience. Second, each aspect of play, as it evolves, becomes more elaborate and tends to combine into more complex events in which two or more resources are used simultaneously —as in rope jumping, which usually combines play with motion and play with language. Third, as play develops, its forms become less determined by properties of the materials in the immediate situation and come increasingly under the control of plans or ideas. This last trend was clearly illustrated in my account of the development of object play. Fourth, as a child's world expands to include more people, situations, and activities, these new experiences tend to be incorporated in his play. In analyzing play with language, we have already begun to see how newly acquired rules for conversation are turned to playful uses.

In this chapter we will examine an aspect of play that reflects the child's rapidly developing competence as a member of his society. Features of the social world, and of socially learned and transmitted expectations of the way objects, actions, and people are related, provide the principal resource of make-believe or pretending. This type of play, when it involves recognizable "characters" and plots of story lines, has also been called dramatic or thematic play. It is perhaps one of the most complex kinds of play conducted in childhood, since it is likely to encompass most if not all of the resources at a child's command and to integrate them into a whole. The principle of integration is some notion or idea, often one that can be named by the child, such as "playing house" or "cops and robbers." There are primarily two kinds of social constructs—socially shared views of the way life is—that serve to integrate pretend play. One is an action plan, a sort of blueprint for arranging actions and events into a coherent episode. The other is the role or identity assumed by the pretender. Roles and plans are intricately interrelated, but it is useful to distinguish them as different kinds of social construct. Indeed, some pretending exhibits a coherent plan without discernible social roles, whereas other pretending appears to rest on adoption of roles with little use of a story line.

It is unlikely that much well-formed pretend play appears before the age of three, and it is generally thought to diminish before adolescence. In an article on the resemblances between imaginative play and private fantasy, Eric Klinger pointed out that "fantasy seems to become frequent after the demise of play."[1] Two somewhat related views have been advanced about the fate of pretending. On the one hand, when overt make-believe play decreases, it may be that make-believing continues but goes underground to become private fantasy or daydreaming. There it is adapted to the characteristic preoccupations of adolescence: popularity, romance, choice of vocation, and achievement of life goals. But at the same time that overt pretend activities decrease in frequency, a different kind of play begins to appear, one that reflects the increasing adaptation of the young person to his social world. Piaget saw the onset of games with rules (especially competitive team games) and the change toward highly realistic symbolic play (such as the construction of elaborately detailed dramas, or inventions of realistic but imaginary countries or epochs) as natural replacements for make-believe.

We will return to questions of the occurrence and functions of pretending at the end of this chapter. But first we must consider the resources available to the child and how they are employed in the service of make-believe.

The linguist Michael Halliday has called the child "one who is learning how to mean."[2] Videotaped records of interactions between parents and children have provided a glimpse of the origins of learning how to mean. The infant's first gestures, whether or not truly responsive and voluntary, are often greeted by the caregiver as if they were intentional. An extension of an arm may be seen as a "reach," and the hand will be grasped; an involuntary grimace may be interpreted as an expression of recognition or pleasure, and the parent will smile back and speak. Similarly, a babbled utterance may be heard as "Mama," and will be immediately repeated or imitated by the mother with considerable pleasure and enthusiasm. The infant may therefore begin to learn how to mean, in the sense of intending or performing purposeful and repeatable acts, by having intention attributed to him. The size of the task that lies ahead of him is immense and hardly conceivable, for so much of what we know and do as human beings in a social world is taken for granted. We are, as Gustav Ichheiser has put it, "blind to the obvious."[3]

Looking at a child's story will strikingly illustrate the features of experience that we tacitly assume we share with others—features of personal relationships, of time, of reference and cause and effect, which a child must presumably acquire as he becomes an accredited human being. The sociologist Harvey Sacks examined the first two sentences offered by a girl (2:9) in response to an invitation to tell a story.[4] *The baby cried. The mommy picked it up.* Built into our interpretation or understanding of these sentences is knowledge of the following obvious but implicit facts. We "know" or surmise that the mommy is the mommy of the baby who cried and that these two individuals belong to or comprise part of a unit we call a family. We know also that the events reported occurred in the same order as the sentences that reported them. Further, we take the first event to be a cause of the second event, and we also feel that the actions described were appropriate and normal. And we can recognize the first utterance as a proper opening for a story, since the initiating event is a problem, a situation that must be resolved or corrected. In some way, the young storyteller was also guided by this same tacit knowledge that allows us to interpret the sentences. Such knowledge is reflected not only in the stories children tell but also, and often in more detail, in their make-believe play.

The social constructs that comprise the resources for make-believe are the child's growing knowledge of classes of individuals and their relationships, of categories and types of goals, and of the possible actions and sequences of action that can be employed to accomplish these goals. To these must be added the "correct" relationship of objects and actions, the expected emotions or attitudes of individuals toward events of various types, and the characteristic combinations of persons and their activities with particular settings and times. The more sophisticated levels of play with objects that develop in the second and third years of life reflect the beginnings of the acquisition and integration of such constructs. Full-scale make-believe presents a still richer and more complex picture of the child's construction of his social world, just at the point when he is learning to take for granted the various aspects of the way this world works.

How, if you were three or four years old, would you go about creating a make-believe play episode with a friend? What kind of knowledge would you have to share? How much of the plan must you make explicit? Are there any ground rules that must be agreed upon? How do you determine the content and the conduct of your pretending?

Adults who may have accidentally or intentionally found themselves engaged in pretending with a child will have noticed that make-believing is not entirely free; one cannot behave *ad libitum*. There are restrictions and, apparently, guidelines for behavior, since a "wrong" move will often be pointed out by the child. One might unknowingly sit down on an imaginary playmate, pour invisible coffee rather than the chocolate syrup on imaginary ice cream, or even forget some essential item of clothing and be told, for example, that *Mommies wear hats*. The Russian psychologist Lev Vygotsky was perhaps the first to emphasize the existence of rules of internal consistency in pretend play and to suggest that spontaneous make-believe often selected and highlighted those features of the world that were most salient to the child at a given time. [5]

WHAT IS MAKE-BELIEVE?

Pretending will be defined here as a voluntary transformation of the Here and Now, the You and Me, and the This or That, along with any potential for action that these components of a situation may have. For such a definition to be workable, one must be able to see when a transformation has taken place, and that is generally achieved by contrasting the transformed with the pre- or post-transformed state. For example, how do we know that a child has adopted the role of wicked witch or working woman? She is most likely to announce her new identity to the playmate, but further she is likely to signal the transformation by speaking in a modified voice, by performing some identifying action, or by moving or gesturing in a manner that contrasts with her normal behavior. Pretending tends to be redundantly marked, and the signals are especially clear at points of transition to and from the pretend state.

One must also be able to tell whether the pretending children can and do distinguish between a situation as it actually is and as they have transformed it. Here, again, the indications are generally explicit. Often, in fact, children discuss features of their immediate or anticipated situation: A: *Is that your firehat?* B: *It's not mine to take home;* or A: *Is this a toy?* B: *No, don't play with it. You might break it.* Reference is also often made to being in or out of a pretend state: *I'm not the dragon anymore. Please don't push me 'cause I'm not the dragon anymore.* We know very little about the criteria children use to distinguish between pretend and what they call "real" or "for real" features of a situation, but there is strong evidence that they believe this to be an important distinction and attempt to apply it appropriately.*

The following example illustrates some of the components of pretending. At the beginning of the excerpt, the girl is holding a baby doll and the boy is watching her put it to bed. At utterance (3) she herself becomes the baby and speaks in a higher-than-normal pitch with whining. The daggers indicate her out-of-baby-role directions to the boy, whose parental role she is prompting. These utterances are produced in her normal speaking voice. At utterance (26) she resumes her own identity and asks a literal question, thus ending the make-believe episode.

Girl (3:3)	*Boy (2:9)*
†(1) Say, 'Go to sleep now.'	
	(2) Go sleep now.
(3) Why? (whining)	
	(4) Baby . . .
(5) Why?	
	(continued)

---

*The child's accuracy in making this judgment on any given occasion, or the degree to which his judgment coincides with that of an adult, is another question. Here I only wish to note that all the participants in the pair sessions could make the distinction "real-pretend" and that its application to their interactions was a matter of immediate concern to them.

†(7) No, say 'Because.'
(emphatically)

(6) Because.

(8) Because!
(emphatically)

(9) Why? Because why?

(10) Not good. You bad.

(11) Why?

(12) 'Cause you spill your milk.

†(13) No, 'cause I bit
somebody.

(14) Yes, you did.

†(15) Say, 'Go to sleep. Put
your head down.'
(sternly)

(16) Put your head down.
(sternly)

(17) No.

(18) Yes.

(19) No.

(20) Yes. Okay, I will spank
you. Bad boy. (spanks her)

†(21) My head's up.
(giggles)

(22) I want my teddy bear.
(petulant voice)

(23) No, your teddy bear go
away. (sternly)

(24) Why?

(25) 'Cause he does. (walks off
with teddy bear)

(26) Are you going to pack
your teddy bear?

This exchange illustrates transformations of identity; the girl acting as Parent becomes Baby and finally resumes her nontransformed identity; the boy becomes Parent. These assumed roles import both actions and attitudes which are represented as characteristic and appropriate to the roles. Baby has been naughty, must be scolded and punished. It won't go to sleep, and its toy must be taken away. Baby whines, the Parent speaks sternly. The most striking aspects of the episode, however, are the extent of engineering provided by the girl and her alternating performance as Baby and as director of the scenario. It appears that, even at the age of three, a child can achieve "role distance," at least with familiar roles such as Parent and Baby.

Another example will illustrate a different kind of make-believe, one that does not depend on transformation of identity. It rests on the creation of a telephone call to which is added a virtuoso enactment of a problem situation. The problem is one of sickness; the solution is care and treatment. The performance is a solitary one by a boy whose companion only subsequently acknowledged the situation the boy had dramatized.

Girl (4:9)	*Boy (4:9)*
	(1) Hey, I have to call my friend Casper. (picks up phone and dials)
	(2) 'Cause he knows Superman's watching him today. (lets phone ring)
	(3) Hello, Casper. How are you doing? (pause)
	(4) What? (gasps)
	(5) Teddy bear got sick? (expression of shock)
	(6) He did? Oh boy! (considerable feeling)
	(7) You know where everything is, right? (slight pause)
	(8) You know where the aspirin is? (slight pause)
	(9) Is he in bed? (pause; (7), (8) and (9) said with more business-like concern)
	(10) Yeah . . . Goodbye, Casper. (hangs up phone and after turning to girl, says seriously)
	(11) I got some bad news to tell you, Kathy.
(12) What?	
	(13) My teddy bear's sick.
	(continued)

(14) Oh. (more polite
than really
concerned)

                  (15) But there's a good thing—
                          My friend Casper is home.

In this episode the boy spoke with an imaginary friend, Casper, who may have been a TV character or just invented for the occasion. The boy's reproduction of telephone gaze (eyes fixed on wall) and pausing to allow his friend to respond were highly realistic. He developed the theme of sickness of a pet and proposed the appropriate treatment and care to Casper. After hanging up, he used a conventional routine to tell his playmate what had happened. Her response was perfunctory, but adequate. Note that the pretend episode was framed—that is, announced in advance and recapitulated and evaluated at the end.

From these two examples, we can see that pretending children use resources from the following categories: (1) roles or identities, which are assigned not only to the immediate participants but also to imagined others; (2) plans for action or story lines, which are often combined to form extended dramas; and (3) objects and settings, which are changed or invented as needed. Carrying out the make-believe is largely a matter of communication.

In order to pretend with a companion, the child needs techniques for indicating who he is, what he is doing, what objects represent (or what objects have been invented), and where he is (at home, at work, on a train). Signals of a play orientation, such as giggling or grinning, are of course available, but not always present in pretend play. Explicit directions to a partner are employed as in the first example, and normative statements are often made, such as *Daddies don't carry pocketbooks* or *Little boys don't drink coffee*. Further, the pretend transformations are mentioned, as in the framing of the second example. In our sessions a great deal of talk was devoted to explicit mention of plans, roles, and objects or settings. Questions, descriptions, and suggestions concerning the various components of pretending are illustrated below:

Component		Example
Role:	self	I'm a work lady at work.
	partner	Are you going to be a bride?
	both	We can both be wives.
Plan:	self	I gotta drive to the shopping center.
	partner	Pretend you hated baby fish.
	both	We have to eat. Our dinner's ready.
Object:	change	This is a train. (putting suitcase on the sofa)
	invent	Now this is cheesecake and this is ice cream. (pointing to empty places on a plate)
Settings		Here we are at the doctor's office.
		This is our house.

In addition to talk about procedures and explicit mention of transformations, another technique for communicating make-believe is enactment. This includes any overt representation by means of content or manner of speech, or content and manner of actions, put forth by the pretender as characteristic of an adopted identity or appropriate for the adopted plan. Pretending to be Baby is enacted by speaking as a baby speaks, saying and doing things a baby would do, reacting to Mommy or Daddy as a baby would, using objects in baby fashion, and expressing babylike needs, desires, and attitudes. Some features of enactment are highly stereotyped; for instance, babies do not (cannot) say "Goo-Goo." Other features of enactment, however, are amazingly realistic. A Mommy, speaking to Baby, shortens and simplifies her utterances; uses terms of endearment; speaks of herself and often uses third-person pronouns for Self and Baby: *That's Baby's food and this is Mommy's food.* She also repeats what she has just said: *Mommy's angry. Yes, Mommy's very, very angry,* and reformulates questions and answers them herself: *Are you tired, Baby? You're tired, aren't you, Baby? Of course you are.* These same characteristics have been widely observed in the speech of adults to very young children.

Some enactments are schematic, representing only salient events in a sequence of actions and omitting details: driving to a store, getting out of a car, getting back in with a milk carton, and returning home—without having parked the car or purchased the milk. Most enactments are clearly created from concepts of appropriate behavior and are most likely not direct imitations of models. For example, a boy who walks into the house announces *Okay, I'm all through with work, honey. I brought home a thousand dollars,* and hands over the money to his beaming Wife has probably not witnessed this scene in his own home. He has, however, generated certain characteristics typical of husbands.

The actual behavior in enactments has been filtered through the child's understanding of his world. Though some enactments consist of purely conventional symbols used to indicate a pretend identity or action, and as such are interesting from the point of view of children's communication, the majority of enactments represent information gained and organized by the child as he learns more and more about the nature of the social world and about himself as part of it.

What are the roles and plans that children have at their disposal? These must differ to some extent across cultures, since they are built on the materials of immediate experience. The major components of pretending were represented among the children we observed, and it is possible to discern some consistent patterns.

IDENTITIES AND ROLES

A pretend space may be populated with various toy animals, people, and imaginary beings. Children can take on the identities of many of these, or can relate to them or talk about them as individuals. The question of animation deserves brief comment, however, before we discuss these role types.

The presence of several large stuffed animals (snake, bear, fish, and a smaller tiger) in the room in our agemate study naturally led to their being animated. Most pairs made the fish swim and the snake wiggle. But more complex than the indication that the snake might slither or bite are those cases in which a child assumed the identity of the animal by speaking for it: *Hello, I'm a baby fish* (said in a high squeaky voice while making the fish swim toward the partner). In another type of transformation the animal was clearly attributed a family role such as Child or Pet, who might also speak or misbehave or require punishment. The stuffed animals could also occupy "functional" roles.

Functional roles are defined in terms of action plans. They are the animate but not necessarily human entities that have specific functions to perform. If, for example, children are engaged in a pretend dinner, both may be diners or one may take the functional role of server. If both are traveling in a car, there must be a driver and a passenger. Functional roles are distinct from family or character roles. A child may simultaneously play a family role such as Mother and the functional role of Cook when preparing a meal.

"Character" roles are of two kinds—stereotyped and fictional. Stereotyped roles are distinguished primarily on the basis of occupation, habitual action, habitual attitude, or personality feature. Examples from our sessions are cowboy, fireman, policeman, Indian chief, bride, wicked witch, doctor, nurse. These types were generally flat in terms of personality, their actions and attributes highly predictable, and their scope of action highly restricted. These characters tended to be associated with appropriate actions, but differed from functional roles in that they could be invoked or adopted without taking part in any action. A boy could say that he wanted to be a fireman or could call a fireman on the phone. A girl could become a bride by putting on a lace curtain, without taking part in a wedding and without having a bridegroom.

Also independent of any specific action was the fictional role. This involved individuals who had proper names and whose source appeared to be stories, television, or oral tradition. Examples are St. George and the Dragon; Santa Claus; Hansel and Gretel; Friedmore Caviters (possibly a TV character, possibly just imagined); Hooey; Cookie Monster; Mr. Donkey; and Dr. Jekyll and Dr. Hines (sic), who were both "good guys." Purely fictive but perhaps only nonce characters were Mrs. Fingernail and Uncle Poop, who had little to offer other than their names, which were considered funny by the children. Few children attempted fictional roles. They were more talked about than enacted. (An exception was a young boy who was either Batman or Robin through the whole session.)

Of great importance were family roles. They usually came in

pairs. One could generally predict, for example, that when a Mommy appeared she would be instantly joined by Daddy or Baby. These roles were treated by the children as if they were always potentially available. They were "there" and needed only to be matched to self or partner or be invoked to be effectively present. These were, of course, Mother, Father, Wife, Husband, Baby, Child (Daughter or Son), Brother, Sister, and much more rarely Grandfather and Grandmother; only one Uncle was mentioned. A Parent, not specifically marked for sex, was sometimes enacted. To be included here is Pet, who was sometimes treated as Child. The stuffed animals were usually drafted for this role.

Family roles can, of course, coincide with functional roles: Mother was usually the server for pretend meals; Father became the defender in the case of danger. Family roles did not coincide with character roles, though they were transformed (reversably) from them. Family roles were stronger than character roles. They were acted out for longer periods of time and, under conditions of transformation, they seemed to be primary; for example, Husband temporarily became a fireman and was then transformed back into Husband.

Transformations occurred across generations but along sex-appropriate lines: Mother → (female) Baby, Daughter → Sister, or Mother → Wife. These roles were always assigned according to the actual sex of each child. A violation of this rule counted as a joke or as an insult and was sometimes used in teasing.

At the fringes of our pretend space, but never on stage, were the peripheral individuals who were discussed or called on the telephone, but whose identity the children never adopted. These were imaginary friends and anonymous guests for whom the house was cleaned and parties planned. Discussions also touched on real but absent people, such as the nursery-school teacher, the third child of the set, or one of the investigators. Their existence was only in the nonplay world, and they did not enter the play space.

Both the sex and the age of the children were factors influencing their choice of which family roles to adopt. As other research findings lead one to expect, boys adopted male roles and girls female roles. This choice was virtually absolute in mixed-sex pairs. In all-male pairs, a few boys adopted some functional role more generally played by girls (like server or shopper) but *never* specified their family role as a female one. In a mixed-sex pair of three-year-olds, a boy who wanted to cook dinner was firmly told by the girl that *Daddies don't cook*. Girls in same-sex pairs were only slightly more versatile, preferring the relational roles of Mother and Child, Wives or Mothers with imaginary children. One girl played doctor to an ailing child, and a good number took on the functional role of repairer (of broken car).

The family role choice was greatly influenced by age. Only Mother, Father, and Baby were enacted by the youngest children, and Mother and Father were also their choices for imaginary telephone partners. Although a few young pairs discussed their "real" siblings and never enacted sibling roles, the older ones talked about Brother and Sister, and occasionally enacted them briefly. They also discussed a few Grandparents and telephoned them several times.

With the increasing age of the pretenders, Baby was replaced by Child, though adult roles were the most favored at all ages. It was not, apparently, much fun to be either Baby or Child. Parents or Husbands and Wives could do more things and could talk more, and Baby or Child was expected to obey and also was liable to be punished or scolded. Two older pairs enacting Mother and Father transformed a stuffed animal to Pet, then to Child. Far more functional and character roles were adopted by the older children as compared to the youngest.

Some functional roles were subject to negotiation, particularly those of driver or passenger in the large wooden car, and driver was preferred. Family roles were often discussed before enactment began. A child assigned the Baby role might declare it was her turn to be Mommy or might bargain for some other role. In one case this was resolved by Mother's inventing an imaginary Baby and her playmate's becoming a nurse. Only among the youngest pairs was a role assignment occasionally rejected outright in favor of the child's own identity. For example, a girl called to a boy *Daddy!* and he replied *I'm not Daddy. I'm Alex.* This response abruptly terminated the interaction. A few minutes later the girl tried again, and again failed to gain a Daddy to complement her own Baby role.

The expansion of the child's world is reflected in these role choices. The youngest children adopted the role that coincided with their actual experience (Baby); or took the *reciprocal* relation to their own experience (Mother or Father). Girls showed much more Mother- or Baby-appropriate behavior than boys, whose Father enactments were less detailed. The older children, however, enacted roles and role pairs that they could not have actually assumed in real life. Not only did they adopt parent roles vis-à-vis an invented or transformed Child, but they represented the relationship, Husband-Wife, or other male-female character roles, and did so in more diverse situations. Husband-Wife roles, however, were drawn in far more detail than were characters (such as the cowboy and the girl; Batman and Cat-Woman).

PLANS

When one child suggests a plan for pretend play, say *We can go on a vacation in a beautiful hotel,* and it is accepted, how do the playmates know what to do next? When a girl shrieks with fear on sighting a stuffed snake, how does the partner know what his actions should be? The majority of the pretend episodes we observed were constructed on a limited number of themes, many of which have been previously reported by other observers in nursery schools. Children seem to have a repertoire of action sequences that can be indicated quite economically and then played out with little discussion of what to do next. I will hypothesize that these themes or action plans are actually constructed by the children, rather than copied or reproduced from some single incident. In enacting relational roles, children obviously select characteristic attributes observed in many different situations and over an extended period. They also "invent" actions or attitudes that may never have been directly experienced but appear to have been inferred from what they know of "real life." Action plans are built up in much the same way.

A plan consists of a sequence of events or actions performed or experienced by a cast of functional roles. The events or actions are associated with characteristic settings and props. A popular plan in the sessions was TREATING-HEALING. The functional roles were patient, healer (who often though not always was identified as doctor), and, optionally, adviser or counselor; the setting was sometimes specified as a doctor's office, sometimes unspecified. The instruments of treatment were transformed or invented props such as a thermometer, medicine, or even food. A school lunchbox in the room served in this plan as a doctor's bag (though in other plans it served as a workman's toolbox or as a lunchbox for Father). The initiating cue that triggered this plan was an announcement of illness, wounds, injury to an animal, or even the death of the Pet. The next step was treatment, which generally led to healing or recovery. The most dramatic announcement was depicted by a girl (5:0) who fell weeping upon her dead Pet (stuffed bear) and cried *He's dead.* Her mother (5:2) solicitously suggested that she give it lots of food and it would come alive again. Despite several attempts, the patient failed to respond to treatment.

The forty-eight acquainted pairs produced fifty-one episodes of a plan we can call AVERTING THREAT. A number of anthropologists and folklorists have also noted the popularity of this theme, even up to age twelve and beyond. The sequence of events for the plan as it developed in our sessions can be divided into three major components:

(1) *Identification of functional roles*
   Source of threat identified (*Here comes a monster*).
   Particular danger noted (*He's going to eat us*).
   Other functional roles (defender and victim) are assigned or enacted. Both children can be victims—both may shriek and flee—or one can be victim and the other defender. Denial of threat is possible (*He won't hurt us*).
(2) *Defense*
   Counteraction by defender (*I'll kill him*).
   Instruments employed (defender may throw dynamite, transformed from toy flashlight).
   Reinforcements can optionally be summoned (*Call our friend the bear to help*).
(3) *Outcome*
   Threat succeeds (*He ate me, I'm dead*).
   Threat is destroyed (*I got him*).
   No clear outcome can be determined.
   A destroyed threat can revive and, if so, the action returns to the first step and recycles again.

An example of an episode built on this plan is taken from a mixed-sex pair. They were at home and in the family roles of Husband (5:0) and Wife (5:2). A fire (source of threat) broke out in the house. The Wife (victim) announced it, and the Husband (defender) extinguished the fire with a hose (stuffed snake, transformed) and provided water noises. The threat then revived as the fire broke out in another part of the house and was again destroyed. It then revived and spread to the sky, whereupon God became the potential victim and the defender (still the boy) had to enlist the help of the "magical" fire snake to destroy the threat. The stuffed animal was transformed again to meet this extraordinary danger.

There were differences in children's performances that related both to age and to sex. Younger pairs were more often both victims, less often defended, and used fewer instruments. Older pairs, even when both members were initially victims, more often introduced a defender. In mixed-sex pairs, it was far more likely that the boy would defend. Only the older children called in reinforcements, and they succeeded in destroying the majority of the threats they faced. In general, these patterns resemble the narrative structures of the stories that children tell.

Other popular plans named by the children which seemed to have the property of unfolding action by action, without extensive discussion of what to do next, were PACKING; TAKING A TRIP; SHOPPING; COOKING; DINING; REPAIRING (anything could be declared broken and then fixed, but the wooden car was most often the object of attention); and TELEPHONING. Each plan had its own inventory of functional roles, and each was carried out alone or combined with other plans to form longer sequences, as when first the car was packed and then the couple drove off on a holiday trip. One basis on which longer sequences are formed appears to involve the interaction of plans and roles.

ROLES, PLANS, OBJECTS

If two children agreed on the assignment of family roles, a number of plans could be joined in a relatively coherent sequence. A pair of three-year-old girls adopted the complementary roles of Mommy (M) and Baby (B). These roles provided a scaffold for several plans and actions. In barest outline these were: M feeds B; M interrupts B's play at stove and warns B to stay away from it; M asks B if she wants to go along to grocery store (when B decides not to go, M drives off alone to buy bread, butter, and milk); a tiny chest of drawers triggers an episode of ironing B's imaginary clothes; B whines and needs to go to bathroom and M takes B to toilet (three-legged stool with glass center); M gives B a toy car (short out-of-role incident as B drives car); M sets table for lunch (out-of-role while M examines toolbelt); B soils her pants; M gives B lunch; M dresses B to take her to Sunday school; B soils her pants again and M prepares to change her. With only a few momentary distractions the two stayed in role for the duration of the fifteen-minute session.

The correct or acceptable selection and execution of plans is a major factor in role enactment. Greater elaboration and more coherent sequencing of plans was observed for familiar roles than for those which the child had not experienced directly (fireman). The relations that hold between roles and action plans require far more systematic study.

Objects in sight also influence the roles that are adopted or assigned. Dress-up clothes certainly suggest further apropriate enactment, and objects appear to trigger the adoption of some plans. Seeing a stove probably increased the likelihood that the children would decide to cook dinner. A miniature toolset often led to the decision that the car needed repair. But the relationship is not always so direct. A pair engaged in AVERTING THREAT succeeded in destroying the monster (snake) by putting him in the oven. The presence of toy telephones in the room probably triggered the large number of telephone calls (eighty-two in all). However, once a plan was embarked upon, object and setting transformations tended to be subject to the requirements of the plan. The observation room or some part of it became a forest, Puerto Rico, a doctor's office, a beach, or a home, as needed.

An enthusiastic and imaginative pretender tends to make do with what is available. A toy flashlight can be tried out as such, but if an instrument is needed to destroy a threat, the flashlight can serve as a pistol or even as a firehose. It is possible to account for many object transformations that might at first seem arbitrary by considering the plan context in which they take place. In carrying out the AVERTING THREAT plan these additional object transformations were made:

(1) Stuffed bear animated as defender.
(2) Stuffed snake animated as source of threat.
(3) Hand became firehose (treated as instrument).
(4) Hand became gun (instrument).

(5) Stuffed snake became firehose (instrument).
(6) Flashlight became dynamite (instrument).
(7) Three-legged stool with magnifying glass became spyglass (auxiliary instrument for spotting fire).

The requirements of the plan or role control the specific transformations that can be made. We have seen that, in the early stages of play with objects, pretending is tied to the perceptual or physical properties of objects. It seems to be the case, however, that once a child reaches a level of cognitive maturity that permits him to operate with roles and plans, he becomes less dependent in his pretending on the real properties of objects. As to the social dimension of pretending, certain props or settings that suggest or permit group activities in which functional roles can be differentiated, such as stores (clerk and customer) or buses (driver and passengers), can encourage social as opposed to solitary play among three or more children.

HOW PRETENDING RELATES TO INDIVIDUAL AND CULTURAL DIFFERENCES

Differences among children in their tendency to engage in imaginative play with roles and plans have been positively related, by means of observation, interviews, and specialized tests, to a number of important cognitive and personality factors. Jerome Singer and his associates have suggested that some children have a stronger predisposition to fantasy than others do.[6] Singer suggests that this "fantasy predisposition" is associated with certain characteristic styles of thinking and feeling. Children rated high on fantasy predisposition tend to enjoy play more, are able to concentrate longer on a single task, and show more self-control while waiting or in submitting to rules. They also produce more numerous and more imaginative ideas. They tend to be divergent thinkers. Divergent production, we have seen, is the generation of novel as opposed to stereotyped responses to problems or situations and is itself characteristic of creative persons. Although a high fantasy predisposition is not directly related to superior intelligence, engaging in make-believe appears to contribute to the flexibility with which a child can approach situations and tasks. Brian Sutton-Smith has suggested that play may heighten the ease with which new approaches or ideas can be adopted toward diverse materials.[7] The imaginative pretender has the experience of manipulating, recombining, and extending associations between words and things, and between things, persons, and actions. Thus it is reasonable to speculate that pretending is one of the experiences that facilitate the development of abstract thought.

Many studies of play in nursery schools in the United States and Europe have reported on the frequencies of pretend play (as opposed to rough-and-tumble or construction activities). Most have also noted girls' preferences for domestic themes and boys' for plans involving transportation or adventure. Researchers have generally agreed that, as children grow and mature, their enactments become more realistic, and their themes or plans are integrated and developed in more complex ways.

There is evidence that a high fantasy predisposition is linked with creativity, that more highly elaborated kinds of imaginative play with roles and plans reflect higher levels of development, and that the content and type of pretend play reflect social experience. The question has been raised whether "sociodramatic" play actually appears in certain cultures or subcultures—a reasonable question, since its free exercise depends on some degree of adult cooperation in providing the time, space, enough privacy, access to props, and, at the minimum, no strong disapproval of make-believing. Thus the home environment probably influences the degree to which children engage in make-believe. Since we also assume that the techniques used in pretending, and the ideas incorporated in it, are products of social learning, the degree to which children create such play may differ along cultural or subcultural lines. The answer is that it does indeed vary across groups.

Anthropologists have reported some cultures in which virtually no make-believe play was observed, but they note make-believe in other non-Western societies, such as the !Kung in the Kalahari. Play themes found in different groups tend to reflect activities important to the particular culture. The children of Hopi Indian settlements, for example, conduct pretend rabbit hunts and play at modeling pottery. Differences in the amount of sociodramatic play among children of different ethnic backgrounds in Israel have been observed in separate studies by

Sarah Smilansky and by Dina Feitelson.[8] They found that young children of Middle Eastern, North Arabic, or Kurdish Jewish immigrants showed comparatively little make-believe. Smilansky argues that its relative absence resulted from family conditions and attitudes and was also associated with a depressed development of cognitive, social, and verbal skills. But on the basis of a large-scale study of the playground and after-school activities of children (aged six to fourteen) in town, village, and kibbutz, from both Jewish and Arabic families, Rivka Eifermann disputed Smilansky's interpretation and claimed rather that make-believe with social themes was not absent, but simply appeared at a somewhat later age in the less advantaged groups.[9]

Separate studies in three eastern cities in the United States have shown that children of lower socioeconomic groups engage in little pretend play, at least in the nursery schools where they were observed. As in the previously cited studies, differences in the children's ages, in observation procedures, and in definitions of the categories of behavior prevent strict comparison among these investigations. Further, one of these studies, by Joan Freyberg, found children with both high and low fantasy predispositions within the lower socioeconomic groups. Freyberg, was able to interview six families of children exhibiting high fantasy and low fantasy characteristics and found very different family profiles for the two types of children. Her results, though based on a small number of cases, suggest that parental support is an important factor in the development of a predisposition to make-believe.[10]

There is, however, another relevant question: Can training, primarily tutoring by an adult, lead children to increase and elaborate this type of play? Here the answer is again a guarded yes. By providing role-playing models, suggesting relations between roles and plans, proposing imaginative situations, and using evocative toys over a period of time (usually at least a month with daily contact), an adult can help children to develop some of the skills needed for make-believe.

The next question, of course, is whether such training and its immediate outcome of more spontaneous pretend play produce significant gains on the tests that measure other important cognitive or social skills. What abilities does training or practice in make-believe promote? The methods of training and modeling that emphasize group activity and the communicative aspects of pretend play have been shown to increase children's cooperative behavior and to contribute to better performance on team problem-solving or construction tasks. Such training also leads to more sensitive role-taking behavior (for instance, selecting appropriate gifts for different members of the family). Modest increments in originality and creativity have been reported after tutoring in imaginative play with toys, dolls, and toy settings. Some increases in verbal skills and language use have also been found after training in sociodramatic play.

Finally, and perhaps most critically, if such gains are shown immediately after training, do they have any lasting effect on the child's subsequent development? There is very little evidence on this question. Freyberg found that, two months after training and testing, the tendency toward increased make-believe play was still evident. Other follow-ups have not been reported.

In conclusion, play with social materials is a reflection of the child's growing notions of his world. Knowledge of the behavior and attitudes appropriate to each sex, though limited of course, has been independently confirmed by other studies of children as young as two and a half. Also there is growing evidence that children of three years of age are aware that others may have attitudes and expectations different from their own. Study of social make-believe shows that the differentiation of self and other, and the behavior appropriate to socially identified persons, classes of objects, and types of goals and plans, are explored and are played with in ways that can be systematically studied.

Roles, plans, and objects are the materials of pretending, and a child can enter the pretend world through any of these means. He can decide to be Daddy and then search for a toolbox and decide to repair the car. Or he can sight a toolbelt and begin to fix the car or imaginary roof, without specifically transforming his identity. Or he can accept the role of Daddy assigned to him by another child, prepare to go off to work, and only then decide that a lunchbox must be taken along. When two or more children pretend together, communication becomes a critical factor in the successful production of make-believe. And in the social conduct of pretending we can see the extent to which children conceive of the family as a system of relationships and as a complex of reciprocal actions and attitudes. Since make-believe enactments and themes reflect the child's notions of his world (though they do not copy them exactly), this aspect of play can provide a rich field for students and observers of social development.

Opposite: !Kung girls dancing the springhare dance (Richard Lee/Anthro-Photo).

7 / Play with Rules

The title of this chapter has two meanings. There is ambiguity in some of the preceding chapter titles as well, but here, specifically, each possible reading refers to a topic that will be discussed below. "Play with rules" can mean that rules accompany or characterize the play. It can also mean that the resource with which the player is engaged is a rule or some sort of limit or constraint. Proponents of Piaget's classification of play into stages have selected the former meaning. According to Piaget, the third and most mature of the stages of play to emerge is "games with rules"—organized, often competitive or team activities, structured by rules that specify the participants and obligate and prohibit moves in the conduct of the play.

I have tried to maintain a distinction between the terms play and game in this book.* The topic has been play, defined as a special subjective orientation to resources. This nonliteral orientation can result in various kinds of playful behavior, many of which resemble activities that can also be carried out in a non-playful fashion (chasing, preparing supper, arguing). But the play behavior I have described, though it is often orderly, internally consistent, and subject to regulation and procedural corrections by the participant (*Your turn* or *You have to wear a hat*

---

*This semantic problem pervades the literature on play. In French, German, and Russian, one word (*jeu, Spiel,* and *igra*) refers at once to both play and game. Translators of the influential works of Jean Piaget and Roger Caillois, for example, must deal with the problem and are sometimes inconsistent in the English words they select. And we ourselves do not, of course, always use "play" and "game" consistently in everyday language to distinguish the different concepts.

or *No, my name is Mr. Caviters, I'm your husband*), lacks certain gamelike characteristics. Games are play activities that have become institutionalized (perhaps in the distant past, perhaps more recently). Childhood games are structured by explicit rules that can be precisely communicated; games can be taught and learned. Their existence depends on acceptance of and adherence to a particular set of rules. Infractions usually carry specific penalties or sanctions. Further, games tend to have traditional names (Drop-the-Handkerchief or Capture-the-Flag), though the names vary across communities and across time. Games have the quality of "social objects"—that is, a game has a clear beginning and end, and its structure can be specified in terms of moves in a fixed sequence with a limited set of procedures for certain contingencies. Thus performances of the same game will be very similar. A particular situated performance can be recalled, talked about, evaluated, or planned in advance. Games, then, are more formal, conventionalized events than are the incidents of spontaneous play. And rules are the essence of games.

This book has not dealt with games, either those that are selected, arranged, and supervised by teachers or parents, or those that are freely chosen and executed by children without adult direction. (Iona and Peter Opie, who studied the games of schoolchildren in Great Britain, have concluded that players overwhelmingly prefer their own games and also that adult-directed games are less favored than those learned directly from other children.[1]) Organized play with games seldom appears (in our culture, at least) until children enter kindergarten or elementary school at five or six. Developmental theory would attribute its appearance at that time to the emerging abilities of the schoolchild to engage in sustained cooperative and competitive social interactions; to plan and to carry out longer and longer sequences of purposive activities; and to exercise self-control and submit voluntarily to restrictions and conventions. These emerging capabilities rest, of course, on the reciprocal interaction of the child's experiences with his physical, cognitive, and emotional growth. Few researchers have studied the beginnings of play with games or have related the games of childhood to the more spontaneous kinds of play described in the preceding chapters.

It is possible that the games with rules of later childhood actually have their roots in the earliest playful experiences of infancy. Perhaps the notion of playing by the rules can be traced to the repetitive and predictable patterns that children learn in their interactions with adults. Jerome Bruner and his associates have studied a number of mother-infant pairs, observing how initial regularities in procedure evolve into rule-structured events.[2] Most of the pairs played Peek-a-Boo. Peek-a-Boo shows clear differentiation of participant roles and an internal structure comprised of moves apportioned between the players. Each repetition of the game rests on the same sequence of moves, though certain variants in the execution of each move are permitted. What makes a good game of Peek-a-Boo is the mutual respect of each participant for the rules—that is, their shared expectations concerning what happens next and their willingness to conform to the agreed-upon procedures.

An outline of the essential structure of the game in its developed form is presented below. This form is usually achieved by the time the child is about a year old.

Initiator's turn		*Recipient's turn*
Round 1:		
Move 1	Attract R's attention	Give attention to I
Move 2	Hide object, self, or R, optional vocalization	Look for
Move 3	Reveal	Appreciate
Move 4	Reestablish contact	Reestablish contact
	(simultaneous)	

Round 2:
Optional repetition of the whole game, with or without permissible variations

Younger children are usually the recipients, but after the first year many children take the initiator role, hiding self or mother. Permissible variants include vocalizations, changes in who or what is hidden, and what is used to conceal the hidden person or object.

These observations suggest that games with rules have a natural history that begins with the first experiences of the social world. A child needs help from others in learning how to join a game and in discovering the pleasures that can be derived from rule-structured activities. At first, supportive adults provide the controlled variation of timing and movements from which he begins to derive his notion of rule-governed events. The first "team" is usually composed of infant and adult, and cooperation in producing the alternating or simultaneous moves of a game is the basic principle to be learned. Only much later will the child be able to enter into games with less familiar persons, and then only if his playmates also know and respect the rules.

The first successful peer games are likely to be cooperative ones, like Ring-around-the-Rosies. Games based on competition —where one team or person strives to win or to defeat the other —become popular somewhat later, at about seven to nine. Although a younger child is at times contentious and tries to rival a playmate's claims or actions (*I'm stronger than you are*), the demands of organized, competitive play are too much for him. To be forced to give up a turn, to lose an object, to accept the status of loser, are difficult experiences. The child will learn to accept such conditions only when his desire to excel is strengthened and supported by the opinions and reactions of his peers.

That rules themselves can be the resource for play is the second meaning of my chapter title. Violating a convention, upsetting an expectation, or taking apart things that should go together—all can be factors in most of the types of play already discussed. One example of enjoyment in using an object incongruously is provided by a boy of two who delighted himself by trying on a hat, then putting a sand bucket upside down on his head, and finally topping himself with one of his father's large rubber galoshes. In fact, Bruner has aptly described play as "a special way of violating fixity."

There is an aspect of play, however, that takes rules, limits, or constraints as the focal material. Risking the consequences of transgressing the boundaries of the permissible or the possible appears to be the source of pleasure. Such play has been described primarily in its adult manifestations. Roger Caillois included "chance" as one of the basic psychological factors that motivate play and games.[3] Erving Goffman, in an article entitled "Where the Action Is," pointed out the fascination with testing limits, taking chances, and running risks (as, say, in gambling or skydiving).[4] If this attraction becomes obsessive, revocability and freedom are lost, and the orientation ceases to be playful.

How do children play with rules and limits? Some familiar examples will indicate the diversity of constraints that can be challenged by school-age children. Testing the limits of one's abilities is the basis for many games of skill. In playing Statues, children attempt to hold the position in which they have fallen as long as is physically possible. In Follow-the-Leader, there is physical challenge (walking on top of a wall, jumping ditches) and an element of psychological daring as well. Inviting fear, and giving over to it, is pleasurable as long as the child "knows" that the situation is manageable or that he is ultimately in control. Voluntary submission to frightening experiences (sometimes called "thrill seeking") underlies the popularity of ghost stories, roller coasters, and monsters, from the Barong of Bali to our own Frankenstein.

Testing the limits of what another person will tolerate is also common; the danger in this case is precipitating a serious breach of friendship. Consequently, this type of play is often ritualized, so that its nonliteral force is made clear. William Labov has described the ritual insults created by black adolescents in New York.[5] What is said is outrageous and often vicious (*Your old man so poor your family have to paint the furniture on the wall*), but the semantic and syntactic structure of the insults marks them as different from nonplay assaults. These attacks generally follow the formula: addressee's relative (mother, father) is so X that Y, where X is derogatory (old, ugly, dirty) and Y is some unpleasant consequence (*Your mother so old she fart ashes*). The insult must be patently false; if it comes too close to the truth the victim could interpret it as literal and take offense. But a "good" ritual insult is understood as such, and the victim then retaliates in kind.

Among the children in our pair sessions, two major types of limits or constraints were playfully challenged. One type might be called prohibitions by adults—either inferred or invented. We did not tell the children they had to stay in the observation room; on the contrary, the opportunity to explore it was presented as a treat. Nevertheless, several played as if it were forbidden to open the door. Two would take turns opening the door, peeking out, then closing the door abruptly and running to the other side of the room *as if* they did not want to be caught at the "naughty" act. The play was accompanied by whispers and giggles. Similarly, several children noticed the microphone hanging from the parrot's perch and seemed to know that it was adult property rather than a toy. So an inferred prohibition was violated by several boys who stood on the car and pretended to touch the microphone. Some partners thought this was funny; others were somewhat uneasy.

The second type of constraint that was playfully violated involved the relations between the children themselves. Some teasing did occur, mostly of a good-natured variety. But taunting someone is always dangerous. In breaking the rules of interpersonal conduct, the aggressor risks a serious fight. In our sessions, one child would taunt another to a point where we, as observers, felt that the victim was about ready to take offense. Then the aggressor would desist, sometimes spontaneously, sometime in response to a warming issued by the victim in a nonplay tone of voice: *If you do that again, I won't be your friend.* A girl (5:0) teased her male partner (4:9) by repeatedly calling to him, *Goodbye, Mother.* In spite of his protests (*I'm not a girl. You're the Mother*), she persisted, apparently pleased with his distress. At last, almost in tears, he stopped her by saying *I will tell on you.* A boy (5:1) teased a girl (5:2) by "stealing" her pans and cooking utensils one by one and hiding them. For a while she pretended to be angry and retrieved each one, but finally when he announced *I stealed your cake* she terminated the episode by saying *I don't care. It's not a cake anymore.* Among the acquainted pairs, teasing never quite exceeded the tolerable limits. In a few unacquainted pairs, teasing led to real unpleasantness, perhaps accidentally, perhaps intentionally.

Play with rules, in both senses of the term, appears at an early age, becomes increasingly complex, and combines with the other aspects. We can speculate that by playfully violating conventions or testing limits—especially those imposed by the consensus of the peer group—a child not only extends the knowledge of his own capabilities but also learns about the nature of social rule systems. Since societies and personalities are both shaped by rules, a better understanding of the beginnings of such play is essential to the study of human development.

8 / Ritualized Play

One of the most interesting features of spontaneous play is ritualization. Rituals, as I use the term, can be based on any resource: motion, object play, language, social conventions; even play with rules can be performed in a ritualized manner. A ritual, then, is defined not by its content or by the resource it builds on, but by its distinctive form: controlled repetition. The nature of the control is generally rhythmic, and the behavior takes on a predictable regularity of tempo. The scale or intensity (as well as the timing) of a performance may also be controlled, so that both the amplitude and frequency of the actions can be grossly exaggerated or sharply attenuated. For example, in the agemate sessions a particular episode of object play performed by several pairs involved the three-legged stool with the magnifying glass. After it had been discovered and its particular property explored, most children would fetch different objects, place them one by one under the glass, and look at the distorted images, invariably finding the result amusing. But one pair created a ritual out of this experience. One boy placed a hat under the glass and said dramatically *That's the biggest hat I ever saw in my life!* His partner said *Let me see,* looked, smiled, and sat back. Then the first boy put his hand under the glass and said *That's the biggest hand I ever saw in my life!* with exactly the same timing and intonation as before. The partner repeated his request and the same movements, then looked expectantly at the leader, who reproduced his part with a different object but with the identical gestural and verbal rhythms. In this chapter I will describe some of the structural characteristics of ritual play, treating ritualization as a feature that can be added to the various types of play.

An example based on play with a conversational convention (for instance, trying to support a contradictory response or a reaffirmation of a statement) will illustrate the timing features of ritual play. The extreme regularity of each exchange would be far more strikingly displayed by an audio recording, but the timing (in seconds and tenths of seconds) of each utterance and each pause between speakers will indicate the precise regulation of behavior that each child achieved. Throughout this ritual, there was no direct gaze. The boy faced the girl, but she did not look at him.

The content is repetition of a fairly common type of exchange, an assertion and counterassertion or contradiction. Thus the basic resource is play with language. But it is the form and timing that mark this example as a ritual. The pause between speakers is a little longer than might be expected in a normal conversational version of this kind of exchange. Here the pause seems to count as a beat in the rhythm. Throughout the ritual proper (which began after utterance 2) the interspeaker pause varied between 0.5 and 0.7 seconds. The length of each speaker's utterances is also remarkably regular. The girl's and the boy's utterances vary between 0.9 and 0.5 seconds. There also seems to be a relationship between the lengths of the utterances: both speakers first speed up, then both lengthen their utterances in approximately the same way as the ritual progresses. The mood of the ritual is not argumentative; the delivery might be called singsong. There is a progressive rise in pitch throughout and a slight decrease in loudness until the last exchange is almost whispered.

Rituals can be created from almost any kind of content. A nonverbal ritual built on alternating physical gestures was conducted by a boy and girl. They had discovered the net curtains, inspected them, and discussed just what they might be (to make tents? to wear?). Then the boy said *Watch this*, and threw a curtain up over his head. As it floated down, he giggled. The girl then said *Watch this*, and did the same thing. They alternated turns, each beginning with an announcement and ending with giggles, and each attended to the other's turn in the action. There were four pairs of turns. Finally the boy concluded the episode by saying *I'm tired*.

Girl (3:6)	Length of utterance	Interspeaker pause	Length of utterance	Boy (3:7)
(1) . . . no, you're already at the snakes.	—	1.2	1.2	(2) No I'm not. (sitting on car)
RITUAL:				
(3) You are too. (ironing)	0.9	0.6	0.9	(4) No I'm not.
		0.6		
(5) You are too.	0.5	0.6	0.5	(6) No I'm not.
		0.7		
(7) You are too.	0.5	0.6	0.5	(8) No I'm not.
		0.5		
(9) You are too.	0.5	0.5	0.5	(10) No I'm not.
		0.5		
(11) Yes, you are too. (wanders across room)	0.5	0.6	0.6	(12) No I'm not.
		0.6		
(13) Yes, you are too.	0.7	0.7	0.7	(14) No I'm not.

(continues through two more exchanges)

This ritual serves to introduce the terms needed for an analysis of more complicated ritual structures. Each person's contribution is called a "turn." This unit of behavior appears to have psychological validity in the sense that, if one person fails to take his turn within the time provided by the rhythm of the ritual, the partner will point out his failure: *You go next* or *Your turn.* In this simple ritual one pair of turns constituted a "round."

> Boy's turn: *Watch this.* (throws curtain, giggles)
> Girl's turn: *Watch this.* (throws curtain, giggles)

The round also appears to have psychological validity as a unit since if a partner suggests *Let's do that again* or *Want to do it again?* a pair of turns (the whole round) is repeated. Features of timing also support the validity of these units.

The content of the curtain ritual is basically motion—throwing curtains up and allowing them to drift back down on top of the head. The phrase *Watch this* marks the focus of action for each turn, and the giggles mark the end of the turns. Since the content of each turn is identical, this type of turn pattern is designated as A-A. The specific content of the turn does not matter; it is classed as A-A if the second child's turn duplicates the content of the first child's. Thus a verbal ritual composed of the identical turns (*Hi, Mommy—Hi, Mommy*) has A-A type content.

A more complicated round can be composed of two turns, where the second turn contains a "paradigmatic" substitution— that is, it substitutes an item from the same class as the first. This sort of relationship would be designated A-B_p (the subscript p denotes a paradigmatic substitution). Examples would be: *Hi, Mommy—Hi, Bubba; —It's blue—It's green.* In the first case, a name was substituted; in the second, an adjective.

But rounds rather than turns are the building blocks of rituals, and the way in which one round follows another must also be distinguished. Thus, a simple ritual starting with an A-B_p round could go on to repeat that round in identical form or could modify it in some way. A ritual composed of three identical rounds (R_i) is:

	Round type	First child	Second child	Turn content type
Round 1	R	Hi, Mommy.	Hi, Bubba.	$A\text{-}B_p$
Round 2	R_i	Hi, Mommy.	Hi, Bubba.	$A\text{-}B_p$
Round 3	R_i	Hi, Mommy.	Hi, Bubba.	$A\text{-}B_p$

A still more complex relationship may be formed from a possible response to the first turn (for example, *You're a girl.—No I'm not.*) rather than from a substitution of an item from the same class (*I'm a monkey.—I'm a donkey.*). The possible response could be verbal, or it could be some nonverbal gesture that could normally complement or complete the content of the first turn. This type of content relationship, which creates a possible conversational sequence, is called "syntagmatic," and such a turn content is coded $A\text{-}B_s$. In the following example, rounds composed of $A\text{-}B_s$ type content are repeated identically (R_i):

	Round type	First child	Second child	Turn content type
Round 1	R	You're a girl.—No I'm not.		$A\text{-}B_s$
Round 2	R_i	You're a girl.—No I'm not.		$A\text{-}B_s$

Rounds, however, can be modified as they are chained together in an episode. A modified round (R_m) built from syntagmatic turn content was created as one child tried to guess the name of his partner's mother:

	Round type	First child	Second child	Turn content type
Round 1	R	It's Linda.	No.	$A\text{-}B_s$
Round 2	R_m	Adam.	No.	$A\text{-}B_s$
Round 3	R_m	Crocodile.	No.	$A\text{-}B_s$
Round 4	R_m	Fish.	No.	$A\text{-}B_s$

(continued for seven rounds)

So far only symmetrical turns have been illustrated: one turn
per person. Still more complex rounds can be built of nonsymmetrical turns; one person can have two turns to his partner's
one. Rounds composed of nonsymmetrical turn structure can
also be "done again." The following example of a round has syntagmatic content in each turn and also has asymmetrical turn
distribution:

First child	Second child	Turn content type
I'm going to work.	You're already at work.	$A\text{-}B_s$
No I'm not.		C_s

If this round, which is composed of three sequential, syntagmatic turns, were repeated intact, the second round would be coded
R_i. But in fact this ritual was still more complex. The second and
third rounds were progressively changed. Thus they were coded
R_m for modified round:

	Round type	First child	Second child	Turn content type
Round 1	R	I'm going to work.	You're already at work.	$A\text{-}B_s$
		No I'm not.	(pause)	C_s
Round 2	R_m	I'm going to school.	You're already at school.	$A\text{-}B_s$
		No I'm not.	(pause)	C_s
Round 3	R_m	I'm going to the party.	You're already at the party.	$A\text{-}B_s$
		No I'm not.	(pause)	C_s

The modified rounds were related by substitution in an utterance
of members of the same class (*to work, to school*). Thus the
round modification principle was paradigmatic. (The internal
structure of each round, however, was built on syntagmatic turn
relations.)

A complete ritual is provided below with coded analysis. A change of turn patterning occurs after the third round, and this change of format was marked by a slight pause and a distinct shift in pitch and volume. The creators of this ritual were a girl (4:4) and a boy (3:9).

	Round type	Amy	Ben	Turn content type
RITUAL:		(1) I can see this.		
Round 1	R	(3) I can see Ben.	(2) I can't see Amy.	A-B$_s$
Round 2	R$_i$	(5) I can see Ben.	(4) I can't see Amy.	A-B$_s$
Round 3	R$_i$	(7) I can see Ben. (slight pause)	(6) I can't see Amy.	A-B$_s$
Round 4	R$_m$	(9) Can't see Ben.	(8) Can't see Amy.	A-B$_p$
			(10) Can't see Amy. *Trashcan!*	

The ritual proper begins with utterance (2), as Ben, seated on the car, picks up on a comment Amy made while looking into the mirror. The first round is composed of utterances (2) and (3) and their intervening pause. Four rounds are completed before Ben concludes the ritual by breaking the format with the exclamation *Trashcan!* As the ritual begins, the interspeaker pauses become very brief. The longer pause between utterances (7) and (8) coincides with a change in round pattern from R$_i$ to R$_m$ and the change in turn content from A-B$_s$ to A-B$_p$. Within each round, the pitch and stress patterns for each speaker were virtually identical, although the number of syllables each produced was different. When Ben modified the last round with utterance (8), and with it the final pitch direction, Amy copied this change exactly. Further evidence on the temporal cohesiveness of ritual play as contrasted with normal interaction is the fact that on the average this pair spoke once every four seconds throughout their seventeen-minute session; during the ritual, however, they spoke on the average every two seconds.

Rituals have several other interesting features. They are clearly set off from other activities by their characteristic style of production. Transitions to and from other activity are easily identified. Sometimes the rituals are even "framed"; that is, the children clearly signal to each other when one begins or ends. And a ritual can be interrupted for procedural corrections. One child can tell the other what to do, momentarily breaking the rhythm and formal structure. Then the ritual is resumed as if no break had taken place. Sometimes one child asks the other what to do next or requests some information he needs to execute his turn. The following example illustrates both framing and embedded procedural clarification. A girl and a boy were carrying on a desultory conversation as the girl packed the suitcase and the boy inspected and handled the several stuffed animals. He showed the fish to the girl and asked in normal conversational voice *Can you carry this?* She replied in a normal voice. Next he gave the fish to her and said *You can't even carry it.* Then the ritual began. Its nonverbal components are indicated in parentheses; the framing material and the embedded clarification sequence are italicized. The ritual begins with the second clause of utterance (3).

Boy (5:2)	*Girl (5:7)*
(1) *Can you carry this?*	
	(2) *Yeah, if I weighed 50 pounds.*
(3) *You can't even carry it.*	
RITUAL	
Can you carry it by the string?	

(4) Yeah. Yes I can.
(lifts fish overhead by
string)

(5) Can you carry it by the
eye?

(carries it by eye)

(6) Can you carry it by the
nose?

(7) *Where's the nose?*

(8) *That yellow one.*

(9) *This?*
(carries it by nose)

RITUAL
(10) Can you carry it by its
tail?

(11) Yeah.
(carries it by tail)

(12) Can you carry it by its
fur?

(carries it by fur)

(13) Can you carry it by its
body?

(carries it by body)

(14) Can you carry it like this?
(shows how to carry it by
fin)

(carries it by fin)

(15) *I weigh 50 pounds almost,
right?*

(16) *Right.*

This ritual combined both language and motion. The boy's
turns were verbal, the girl's primarily variations of picking up
and carrying the fish. The turn pattern of the seven-round ritual
was A-B$_s$: it was syntagmatic because the girl's actions were
normal responses to the boy's indirect requests for action. The
rounds were symmetrical. Each round was modified (R_m), and
the nature of the round modification was paradigmatic. The suc-
cessive changes in each round were formed by substitution in the
initiating turn, *Can you carry it by X?* where X is successively
string, eye, nose, and so on. Utterances (7) to (9) interrupted
the ritual for a brief check on fact, but the ritual resumed imme-

diately. Utterance (10) had the same intonation as utterance (6). All of the boy's ritual phrases had the same intonation pattern.

Two important trends in the form of rituals across age groups were noted. First, there was a tendency for the older pairs to create the more complex rituals, that is, those with three-turn rounds (asymmetrical rounds) and those with modified rounds. The second trend was the preference of the younger pairs for longer rituals. With minor procedural interruptions and minor format changes, the *Hi Mommy—Hi, Bubba* ritual continued for two minutes.

Repetition and repetition-with-variation have long been recognized as characteristics of early play. They are characteristic also of certain kinds of adult behavior. They constitute a formative principle in magical incantations and spells, religious chants, cheers for football teams, political rallies, riots, in fact many events where members of a group must be synchronized to express solidarity. For children, repetition is apparently enjoyable for its own sake, even in solitude, but in an intimate social situation it provides a basis and framework for continued interaction. In terms of the content, such interaction is relatively inexpensive: no new topics, ideas, or opinions are required. In the rituals each child controls very precisely the behavior of the other, and this regulation is itself satisfying—a form of mastery play, where what is mastered is the control of one's own and one's partner's actions. But these explanations are only speculation—we do not know why children engage in rituals, but we know that they do so and to some extent how they do it.

The study in which pairs of unacquainted children were observed in the same playroom produced rituals also, though somewhat fewer on the average. This kind of social interaction, then, is presumably not unusual, but is probably only rarely produced in nursery schools. Its breeding ground is relatively quiet, undistracted togetherness. What is surprising about the rituals is the extent to which the participants are able to establish and maintain the patterns of exchange, the alternating turns, the sequencing of rounds, and the precise timing. The synchronization of utterance and pause durations indicates a far greater ability to attend to and to adapt to a partner's behavior than has generally been attributed to preschool children.

A ritual is unmistakably play. It exhibits all the descriptive characteristics by which instances of play are recognized. It is apparently enjoyable, performed for its own sake rather than for a goal such as information exchange or the resolution of a disagreement. It is quite spontaneous and engages both partners in precision performances. Rituals are generally based on some other behavior that *could be performed* as nonplay, like peeking out of the door, exchanging greetings, asking and answering questions, and so on. Finally, rituals are very clearly marked as nonliteral by their repetition and by their highly controlled rhythmic execution.

The message, "This is play," is emblazoned on the ritual.

9 / Learning To Play

There is compelling evidence that play is a natural product of the processes of physical and cognitive growth. Is it true, then, that for the normal, healthy, immature creature, play just "happens"? Does the child spontaneously transfer new achievements into the simulative mode? Or must the child learn to play? There are yet no clear answers to these questions. I suggest that most aspects of play will emerge spontaneously *if the very young child experiences some basic model of nonliteral treatment of resources.* As the child matures, the various aspects of play come more and more under the influence of cultural and environmental factors that select and elaborate some kinds of behavior and neglect others.

Current research on interaction between adults and infants indicates that a basic model is amply available. The infant encounters nonliteral behavior that is clearly signaled as such (like tickling) and that contrasts with literal treatment (such as purposeful handling in bathing or changing). Several investigators, notably Judy Dunn, Deborah Rosenblatt, and Meredith West, have observed mothers animating toy animals and pushing miniature vehicles with appropriate engine noises.[1] Young children who are just beginning to move about freely often have their gestures interpreted for them by parents: *Oh, you're helping Mother dust, aren't you?* Thus it seems likely that children do have models from which to derive the *as if* orientation of play, but there is still much to learn about how they generalize this knowledge to produce their own, often original, playful performances.

This book has attempted to show that play takes diverse forms that change and become elaborated as the child matures.

The facts lead to the consensus that it is difficult, if not impossible, to propose any single or uniform function for play in the life of a child or an immature animal. Playing with different resources at different levels of development will obviously have varied functions. Susanna Millar has suggested that the usefulness of play activities is related to their tendency to occur at relatively early stages in the organization of each of the child's systems of behavior.[2] Because playing is voluntarily controlled activity (executed in a way in which imperfect achievement is minimally dangerous), its effects are probably intricately related to the child's mastery and integration of his experiences.

Although playful activities generally derive from nonplay behavior patterns, those patterns need not be mature or complete to serve as a basis for play. They must, however, be sufficiently well controlled to be repeated, varied, and performed in such a way that their intent is signaled: the nonliteral orientation must be communicated. To say that play rests on the nonplay repertoire of behavior does not imply that the influence is necessarily unidirectional. A behavior pattern performed in the simulative mode can be elaborated and combined with other similarly "displaced" patterns. When the behavior is next performed in a nonplay mode, it may be more skilled, better integrated, and associated with a richer or wider range of meaning. In this way play can contribute to the expertise of the player and to his effectiveness in the nonplay world.

Finally, play has considerable value for students of child development. Some uses are obvious. For example, the changing forms of play, which tend to reflect newly acquired abilities, are associated with the course of normal growth and maturation. The failure of play to evolve—to become more complex and differentiated—often signals the existence of developmental problems. Less obvious, however, is that the study of spontaneous play can provide a rich source of information about the nature of a child's competence. Children at play enact or represent knowledge of their social and material world they cannot verbalize explicitly or demonstrate in the setting of experimental tasks. As long as *we* do not interpret their behavior overliterally, we can learn much about children's concepts of social rules and obligations, their understanding of the physical environment, and their knowledge of language structure—about all of the critically human resources at their command.

References

1 What Is Play?

1. P. Reynolds, "Play, Language and Human Evolution," in J. Bruner, A. Jolly, and K. Sylva, eds., *Play: Its Role in Development and Evolution* (Harmondsworth: Penguin, 1976).
2. J. Bruner, "The Nature and Uses of Immaturity," *American Psychologist*, 1972, 27, 687-708.
3. C. Garvey, "Some Properties of Social Play," *Merrill-Palmer Quarterly*, 1974, 20, 163-180.
4. J. Piaget, *Play, Dreams and Imitation in Childhood* (London: Routledge, 1951; New York: Norton, 1962).

2 The Natural History of the Smile

1. A. Sroufe and J. Wunsch, "The Development of Laughter in the First Year of Life," *Child Development*, 1972, 43, 1326-1344.
2. F. Justin, "A Genetic Study of Laughter Provoking Stimuli," *Child Development*, 1932, 3, 114-135.
3. L. Sherman, "An Ecological Study of Glee in Small Groups of Preschool Children," *Child Development*, 1975, 46, 53-61.

3 Play with Motion and Interaction

1. Piaget, *Play, Dreams and Imitation in Childhood*, p. 91.
2. D. Stern, "Mother and Infant at Play: The Dyadic Interaction Involving Facial, Vocal and Gaze Behaviors," in M. Lewis and L. Rosenblum, eds., *The Effect of the Infant on Its Caregiver* (New York: Wiley, 1974).
3. I. Eibl-Eibesfeldt, "Concepts of Ethology and Their Significance in the Study of Human Behavior," in H. Stevenson, E. Hess, and H. Rheingold, eds., *Early Behavior* (New York: Wiley, 1967).
4. H. Harlow, "Agemate and Peer Affectional Systems," in D. Lehrman, R. Hinde, and E. Shaw, eds., *Advances in the Study of Behavior*, vol. 2 (London and New York: Academic Press, 1970).
5. M. West, "Social Play in the Domestic Cat," *American Zoologist*, 1974, 14, 127-136.
6. M. Bekoff, "Social Play in Coyotes, Wolves and Dogs," *Bio Sciences*, 1974, 24, 225-230.
7. C. Eckerman, J. Whatley, and S. Kutz, "The Growth of Social

Play with Peers During the Second Year of Life," *Developmental Psychology*, 1975, *11*, 42-49.

8. E. Mueller and C. De Stefano, "Sources of Toddlers' Social Interaction with Their Peers," *Early Child Development and Care* (in press).

9. W. Bronson, "Developments in Behavior with Agemates During the Second Year of Life," in M. Lewis and L. Rosenblum, eds., *Peer Relations and Friendship* (New York: Wiley, 1975).

10. N. Blurton-Jones, "Categories of Child-Child Interaction," in N. Blurton-Jones, ed., *Ethological Studies of Child Behavior* (Cambridge: Cambridge University Press, 1972). P. Smith and K. Connolly, "Patterns of Play and Social Interaction in Preschool Children," in Blurton-Jones, ed., *Ethological Studies of Child Behavior*.

11. W. Nydegger and C. Nydegger, "Tarong, an Ilocos Barrio in the Philippines," in B. and J. Whiting, eds., *Six Cultures: Studies of Child Rearing* (New York: Wiley, 1963).

4 Play with Objects

1. J. Bruner, "The Growth of Representational Processes in Childhood," in J. Anglin, ed., *Beyond the Information Given* (London: Allen & Unwin, 1974; New York: Norton, 1974).

2. M. Lowe, "Trends in the Development of Representational Play in Infants from One to Three Years: An Observational Study," *Journal of Child Psychology*, 1975, *16*, 33-48.

3. G. Fein, "A Transformational Analysis of Pretending," *Developmental Psychology*, 1975, *11*, 291-296.

4. G. Hutt, "Exploration and Play in Children," *Symposia of the Zoological Society of London*, 1966, *18*, 61-81.

5. K. Sylva, "Play and Learning," in B. Tizard and D. Harvey, eds., *The Biology of Play* (London: Heinemann, 1976; Philadelphia: Lippincott, 1976).

6. E. Mueller and T. Lucas, "A Developmental Analysis of Peer Interaction among Toddlers," in Lewis and Rosenblum, eds., *Peer Relations and Friendship*.

7. M. Waterhouse and H. Waterhouse, "Primate Ethology and Human Social Behavior," in R. Michael and J. Crook, eds., *Comparative Ecology and Behavior of Primates* (New York: Academic Press, 1973).

8. Eckerman et al., "The Growth of Social Play with Peers During the Second Year of Life."

9. H. Rheingold and K. Cook, "The Contents of Boys' and Girls' Rooms as an Index of Parents' Behavior," *Child Development*, 1975, *46*, 459-463.

10. M. Parten, "Social Play among Preschool Children," *Journal of Abnormal and Social Psychology*, 1933, *28*, 136-147.
11. E. Erikson, "Sex Differences in Play Configurations of Pre-Adolescents," *American Journal of Ortho-Psychiatry*, 1951, *21*, 667-692.
12. J. and Z. Henry, *"The Doll Play of Pilaga Indian Children* (New York: Vintage Books, 1974).

5 *Play with Language*

1. K. Chukovsky, *From Two to Five* (Berkeley: University of California Press, 1963).
2. I. and P. Opie, *The Lore and Language of Schoolchildren* (Oxford and New York: Oxford University Press, 1959).
3. H. Johnson, *Children in the Nursery School* (New York: Agathon Press, 1972).
4. E. Keenan, "Conversational Competence in Children," *Journal of Child Language*, 1974, *1*, 163-183.
5. R. Weir, *Language in the Crib* (The Hague: Mouton, 1972).
6. Chukovsky, *From Two to Five*, p. 96.
7. A. Davison, "Linguistic Play and Language Acquisition," in *Papers and Reports on Child Language Development* (special issue; Sixth Child Language Research Forum, Stanford, 1974).
8. J. Austin, *How To Do Things with Words* (Cambridge: Harvard University Press, 1962).

6 *Play with Social Materials*

1. E. Klinger, "The Development of Imaginative Behavior: Implications of Play for a Theory of Fantasy," *Psychological Bulletin*, 1967, *72*, 277-298.
2. M. Halliday, *Explorations in the Functions of Language* (London: Arnold, 1973).
3. G. Ichheiser, *Appearances and Realities* (San Francisco: Jossey-Bass, 1970).
4. H. Sacks, "On the Analyzability of Stories by children," in J. Gumperz and D. Hymes, eds., *Directions in Sociolinguistics* (New York: Holt, Rinehart and Winston, 1972).
5. L. Vygotsky, "Play and Its Role in the Mental Development of the Child," *Soviet Psychology*, 1967, *5*, 6-18.
6. J. Singer, ed., *The Child's World of Make-Believe* (New York: Academic Press, 1973).
7. R. Herron and B. Sutton-Smith, eds., *Child's Play* (New York: Wiley, 1971).
8. S. Smilansky, *The Effects of Sociodramatic Play on Disadvan-*

taged Preschool Children (New York: Wiley, 1968). D. Feitelson, "Cross-Cultural Studies," in Tizard and Harvey, *The Biology of Play*.

9. R. Eifermann, "Social Play in Childhood," in Herron and Sutton-Smith, eds., *Childs play*.
10. J. Freyberg, "Increasing the Imaginative Play of Urban Disadvantaged Children Through Systematic Training," in Singer, ed., *The Child's World of Make-Believe*.

7 Play with Rules

1. I. and P. Opie, *Children's Games in Street and Playground* (Oxford and New York: Oxford University Press, 1969).
2. J. Bruner and V. Sherwood, "Peekaboo and the Learning of Rule Structures," in J. Bruner, A. Jolly, and K. Sylva, eds., *Play: Its Role in Development and Evolution* (Harmondsworth: Penguin, 1976).
3. R. Caillois, *Man, Play and Games* (New York: Free Press, 1961).
4. E. Goffman, *Interaction Ritual* (New York: Doubleday Anchor, 1967; Harmondsworth: Penguin, 1971).
5. W. Labov, *Studies in the Black English Vernacular* (Philadelphia: University of Pennsylvania Press, 1972).

9 Learning To Play

1. J. Dunn, "Play at Home," in Tizard and Harvey, eds., *The Biology of Play*. D. Rosenblatt, "The Predictive Value of Play," in Tizard and Harvey, eds., *The Biology of Play*. M. West, private communication.
2. S. Millar, *The Psychology of Play* (Harmondsworth: Penguin, 1968).

Suggested Reading

Owen Aldis, *Play Fighting* (New York and London: Academic Press, 1975). A technical but readable discussion of "play fighting" (rough-and-tumble play) and "thrill-seeking" behavior in children and young animals. Ethological and experimental psychological studies are complemented with the author's own videotaped material of children at playgrounds, zoos, carnivals, and in the streets. Aldis argues that play fighting contributes to the development of emergency skills and that play fear is a natural, pleasurable way of exploring one's emotional reactions to uncommon events.

Jerome Bruner, Allison Jolly, and Kathy Sylva, eds., *Play: Its Role in Development and Evolution* (Harmondsworth: Penguin, 1976). A collection of writings on play from many different sources—scientists, philosophers, artists —organized under four major topics: the evolutionary context; play and the world of objects and tools; play and the social world; play and the world of symbols. This eclectic and imaginative compilation provides an excellent picture of the diversity and pervasiveness of play in nature and in civilization.

Roger Caillois, *Man, Play and Games* (New York: Free Press, 1961). A thoughtful, provocative essay on the nature and functions of play and games in society. The author has attempted to systematize the great range of variation across time and cultures of types of adult play. The emphasis is social-psychological, and the objective is to account for the motivations that underlie play and games and the roles of these phenomena in human societies.

Robin Herron and Brian Sutton-Smith, eds., *Child's Play* (New York: Wiley, 1971). This book provides a clear and interesting account of the ways that play has been studied— from the perspectives of experimental and clinical psychology, anthropology, ethology, and psychotherapy. Groups of papers by authors representative of the various points of view are presented, and each is introduced by an excellent summary of major issues, types of approach, and research results characteristic of the discipline.

Susanna Millar, *The Psychology of Play* (Harmondsworth: Penguin, 1968). A comprehensive and readable introduction to the study of play in animals and young children, which also provides a good introduction (with a slight bent toward Piagetian theory) to this area of developmental psychology. A historical account of theory and a review of current research are related to the author's observations of her own children.

Jean Piaget, *Play, Dreams and Imitation in Childhood* (London: Routledge, 1951; New York: Norton, 1962). One of the best "personalized" introductions to Piaget's unique and influential ideas about the progression from infancy to childhood to adolescence. Although his discussions on the dynamics of development make rather difficult reading, Piaget's text is filled with detailed and fascinating observations of the day-to-day behavior of his own three children, accounts that can assist any parent in understanding and enjoying his own child's progress.

Jerome L. Singer, *The Child's World of Make-Believe* (New York: Academic Press, 1973). A rather technical and detailed review of clinical, experimental, and personality psychology in the area of imaginative play. Singer and his colleagues (several of whose studies are included in this book) have developed research procedures and tests to assess predisposition to fantasy in school-age children and to determine its relationship to other personality features and also to such factors as age, sex, and social class.

Index

Affective-behavioral systems, 6

Age differences: in play with objects, 43-44; in vocalization, 61-63; in pretend play, 80; in choice of family roles, 90-91; in plans for make-believe, 94; in play vs. games, 104; in rituals, 120

Animals: in play with motion, 27-34; experimental dialogue among, 28; in play with peers, 29-34

Austin, John, 75

Beagles, play among, 32

Bekhoff, Marc, 32-33, 36

Blurton-Jones, Nicholas, 36

Bronson, Wanda, 34-35

Brower, Sidney, 56-57

Bruner, Jerome, 6; on modes of experience, 42; on role-structured play, 105

Caillois, Roger, 106

Cats, play among, 29-32

Character roles, stereotyped and fictional, 89

Chukovsky, Kornei, 59, 70

Communication: play among animals as, 29, 33; by showing objects, 52; of make-believe, 86-88

Connolly, Kevin, 36

Conversation, play with, 72-76

Coyotes, play among, 32

Creativity: and object play, 48-51; and fantasy, 97

Cultural differences, and make-believe, 96-98

Darwin, Charles, 3

Davison, Anne, 73

Daydreaming, as late fantasy, 80

Divergent thinking, 48; and fantasy, 96

Dolls, play with, 55

Dunn, Judy, 123

Eckerman, Carol, 34, 53

Egocentrism of preschool child, 9

Eibl-Eibesfeldt, Irenäus, 27

Eifermann, Rivka, 98

Enactive mode, 42

Enactment, as technique of make-believe, 87-88

Episodes in make-believe: treating-healing, 92-93; averting threat, 93, 95; others, 94

Erikson, Erik, 55

Exploration: and play, 28-29; observing as a form of, 37; progression to play from, 46-50

Expressive behavior, with objects, 56-57

Fantasy: in play with language, 70-72; progression of, 80; predisposition to, 96

Fein, Greta, 45

Feitelson, Dina, 98

First-born children, watchful behavior of, 27

Flexibility complex, 28

Freyberg, Joan, 98

Games: vs. play, 103-104; cooperative vs. competitive, 106

Gaze, in young infants, 26

Goffman, Erving, 106

Grasping, prerequisite to exploration, 41